OPERATION GALVANIC

DANIEL WRINN

OPERATION GALVANIC

1943 BATTLE FOR TARAWA

DANIEL WRINN

CONTENTS

Building a relationship with my readers is one of the best things about writing. I occasionally send out emails with details on new releases, special offers, and interesting details I find in my research. If you'd like to be added to my Readers Group, just click here and I'll add you to the list.

Those who were not hit would always remember how the machine gun bullets hissed into the water, inches to the right, inches to the left.

— ROBERT SHERROD, TIME MAGAZINE

INTRODUCTION

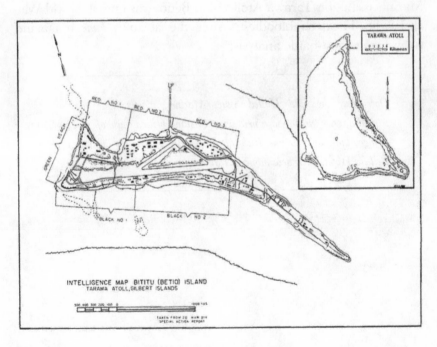

INTELLIGENCE MAP BITITU (BETIO) ISLAND
TARAWA ATOLL, GILBERT ISLANDS

In August 1943, Admiral Spruance, the Central Pacific Naval Force Commander, met in secret with Gen. Julian Smith and other 2nd Marine Division staff officers. Adm. Spruance told the Marines to prepare for an amphibious assault in the Gilbert Islands by November. The Marines were well aware of the Gilbert Islands. Under Colonel Evans Carlson, the 2nd Marine Raider Battalion had attacked Makin only a year before. Intelligence reported that the Japanese had fortified Betio Island in the Tarawa Atoll. Imperial Japanese Marines guarded an airstrip that Adm. Spruance designated the prime target for the 2nd Marines.

Colonel Shoup was Gen. Smith's operation officer. He studied Betio's primitive chart and saw the tiny island was surrounded by a barrier reef. Col. Shoup asked if any of the Navy's shallow draft experimental plastic boats would be provided. He was disappointed to hear that only the usual wooden landing craft would be available for this assault. The operation on Tarawa had become a tactical watershed. This would be the first large-scale test of American amphibious forces against a strongly fortified beachhead. The Marine assault on Tarawa Atoll's islet, Betio, was one of World War II Pacific Theater's bloodiest. After the assault, *Time* magazine published its post-battle analysis:

Over three thousand United States Marines, mostly now dead or wounded, gave the nation a new name to stand behind those of Concord Bridge, the Bon Homme Richard, Little Big Horn, the Alamo, and Belleau Wood. This new name is Tarawa.

THE YOGAKI PLAN

THE GILBERT ISLANDS comprise sixteen scattered atolls along the equator in the Central Pacific. Tarawa Atoll is over 2,000 miles southwest of Pearl Harbor and 540 miles southeast of the Marshall Islands. Betio is the principal islet in the Tarawa Atoll.

Three days after Pearl Harbor, the Japanese seized Makin and Tarawa from the British. After a raid in August 1942, the Japanese realized their vulnerability in the Gilbert Island chain. After the attack, the *6th Yokosuka Special Naval Landing Force* was dispatched to the islands, led by Admiral Saichiro, a well-known engineer. He directed the construction of advanced and sophisticated defensive positions on the Tarawa Atoll. Adm. Saichiro's vision was to make Tarawa so formidable that any American amphibious assault would stall at the water's edge, and allow the Japanese time to annihilate the landing force.

The Japanese strategy was outlined in the *Yogaki* Plan. Its principal point was to defend Eastern Micronesia from an Allied invasion. Admiral Nimitz took the Japanese threat of counterattack with bombers, submarines, and their main battle fleet, seriously. Adm. Nimitz told Spruance, "Get the hell in and the hell out." The overall theme of this island assault was to seize the Gilbert Island targets with lightning speed.

Codename "Operation Galvanic" was assigned by the Joint Chiefs of Staff to capture Tarawa and Makin in the Gilbert Islands. The 2nd Marine Division was given the invasion of Tarawa while the Army's 165th Regimental Combat Team would assault Makin. All three of the landing force commanders assigned to Operation Galvanic had the last name Smith. The senior general was Holland "Howling Mad" Smith, who commanded the V Amphibious Corps. General Julian Smith commanded the 2nd Marines. And General Ralph Smith was in charge of the 27th Infantry Division.

Admiral Kelly Turner, a veteran of the bloody Guadalcanal Campaign, was assigned command of all amphibious assault forces for Operation Galvanic. Adm. Turner was accompanied by Gen. Holland Smith and was given Task Force 52 for the assault on Makin.

Admiral Harry Hill was assigned command of Task Force 53 for the assault on Tarawa. Gen. Julian Smith and Adm. Harry Hill discussed the plans on board the battleship *Maryland*. These two officers couldn't be more different. Adm. Hill was impetuous and outspoken, while Gen. Smith was reflective and reserved. They worked together well and outlined a plan for the assault on the Gilbert Islands. Adm. Spruance set the D-Day for November 20, 1943.

Col. Shoup came up with an outline for tackling Betio's barrier reefs. The Marines used LVT-1s (Landing Vehicle Tracked or "Alligators"), an amphibian tractor, during Guadalcanal. The Alligators were unarmored logistical vehicles. They were not assault craft, but true amphibians—capable of being launched at sea and moving through moderate surf to reach the shore. Col. Shoup discussed the potential idea of using the LVT assault craft with the 2nd Amphibian Tractor Battalion commander, Major Henry Drews. The major liked the idea but warned Shoup that many tractors were in poor condition after the Guadalcanal Campaign. Maj. Drews could provide only seventy-five Alligators—nowhere near enough to transport all the assault waves. Worse, the thin hulled tractors were vulnerable to enemy fire and would need armor plating. Col. Shoup ordered Maj. Drews to modify the tractors with whatever armor plating he could scrounge together.

Gen. Julian Smith knew that the armored LVT-2s, known as "Water Buffalo", were stockpiled in San Diego. He submitted an urgent request for one hundred newer models to be dispatched immediately. Gen. Holland Smith endorsed the request while Adm. Turner disagreed. The argument was intense. Adm. Turner did not dispute the need for Marines to have a reef crossing capability. He objected to the fact these newly ordered vehicles would need to be transported to Tarawa. They'd require LSTs (Tank Landing Ships). The LSTs slow speed (8 knots max) would require an additional convoy, independent escorts, and increased risk of losing the initiative and strategic surprise. Gen. Smith reduced the debate to the essentials:

No LVTs, No operation.

Adm. Turner eventually agreed, but it would not be a complete victory for the 2nd Marines. Fifty of the new one hundred LVT-2s would support the Army's landing at Makin against a lighter opposition. The Marine vehicles scheduled to arrive would not be there in time for any workup training or rehearsal landings. The first time the Marine Infantry would lay eyes on the LVT-2s would be in the predawn hours of Tarawa's D-Day—if at all.

TASK FORCE 53

REPLACEMENT TROOPS POURED into New Zealand. Gen. Smith requested the reassignment of Colonel Edson to be his division chief of staff. The fiery Col. Edson was now a Marine Corps legend for his heroic exploits on Guadalcanal. He worked tirelessly to forge the new recruits and veterans into an effective amphibious assault team. The intelligence reports from Betio were startling. The island was void of any natural fortifications to conceal enemy fire. And too narrow, inhibiting any maneuvering room, which favored the Japanese. Betio was 800 yards at its widest point and less than three miles long. It also contained no natural elevation higher than ten feet above sea level. Col. Edson observed that every place on the island could be covered by machine gun and direct rifle fire.

These elaborate defenses were prepared by Adm. Saichiro. He used minefields, long strings of barbed wire to protect beach approaches, and concrete and steel pillboxes and bunkers. The Japanese built a barrier of coral and logs around much of the islands. They use tank traps to protect fortified command bunkers and firing positions inland of the beach. Of the island's five hundred pillboxes, most were covered by steel plates, logs, and sand.

The Japanese defenders on the island had 8-inch turret-mounted naval rifles, "Singapore guns." They also had many anti-aircraft, anti-boat, heavy caliber coastal defense and field artillery guns, and howitzers. They had an abundant amount of 50mm mortars, dual-purpose 13mm heavy machine guns, and light tanks with 37mm guns. During August, the Japanese high command replaced Saichiro with Admiral Shibasaki, an officer with a reputation for being more of a fighter than an engineer.

Intelligence estimated the total strength of the enemy garrison on Betio was 4,800 men. Twenty-six hundred of them were Imperial Japanese Marines, first-rate naval troops, nicknamed "Tojo's best." Col. Edson's 1st Raider Battalion had taken nearly 100 casualties wrestling Tulagi from these elite Japanese naval troops in the previous August. Adm. Shibasaki boasted that a million Americans couldn't take Tarawa in a hundred years. His optimism was understandable at the time, because Tarawa was the most heavily defended island ever invaded by Allied forces in the Pacific.

Task Force 53 desperately needed detailed tide information. Col. Shoup was confident that the LVTs could negotiate the reef during any tide. Still, the rest of the tanks, artillery, assault troops, and reserve forces would need to come ashore in Higgins boats (LCVPs). The water depth over the reef was four feet, it was enough to float a loaded Higgins boat. If less than four feet, the troops would need to wade several hundred yards ashore against an array of deadly Japanese weapons.

A New Zealand reserve officer, with fifteen years' experience sailing Tarawa's waters, predicted: "there won't even be 3 feet of water on that reef when the assault begins."

Col. Shoup took his warning seriously and made sure that all troops knew in advance that there would be a 50-50 chance of having to wade ashore. Besides the island's physical constraints and daunting Japanese defenses, Col. Shoup proposed a landing plan that included a preliminary bombardment and advance seizure of neighboring Bairiki Islands, to be used as an artillery firebase and a decoy landing. Gen. Smith took this proposal to Pearl Harbor and recommended it to the significant officers involved in Operation Galvanic: Admirals Spruance, Turner and Nimitz, and Gen. Holland Smith.

The restrictions imposed by CinCPac were sobering. Adm. Nimitz declared that the requirement for strategic surprise would limit any bombardment of Betio to only three hours on the morning of D-Day. He also ruled out Bairiki's advance seizure and any decoy landings to defend against the Japanese fleet. To make things worse, Gen. Holland Smith announced that the 6th Marines would be withheld and used as a reserve force. The 2nd Marine Division's tactical options had been stripped away. Ordered into a frontal assault against the teeth of Japanese defenses on Betio with only a three-hour bombardment. Without the 6th Marines attacking the island fortress, that would mean only a 2:1 troop superiority—well below the doctrinal minimum.

Col. Shoup returned to New Zealand and prepared a modified operations order and selected the landing beaches. The southwestern tip of Tarawa near the lagoon entrance looked like the profile of a crested bird lying on its back. The Japanese concentrated their defenses on the southern and western coasts (the bird's head and back). Northern beaches had calmer lagoon waters and only one deadly exception. Defenses in this sector were incomplete, but being improved daily. A thousand-yard pier that jutted north over the fringing reef into deeper lagoon waters (the bird's legs, sticking upward) was an attractive logistics target. He selected the northern coast for landing beaches—but there was no safe avenue of approach.

The northern shore of Betio from the departure line within the lagoon was designated for the three landing beaches, each 600 yards in length. Moving from west to east, Red Beach One, made up the bird's beak and neck from the northwestern tip of Betio to a point just east, Red Beach Two made up the bird's breast from the juncture to the pier, and Red Beach Three from the pier eastward. Green Beach on the western shore, along with other beaches, would be designated as contingencies.

Gen. Smith planned to land with two regiments abreast and one in reserve. Losing the 6th Marines forced him to make a significant change. Col. Shoup's modified plan now assigned the 2nd Marines, reinforced by 2/8 (2nd Battalion, 8th Marines) as the main assault force. The rest of the 8th Marines would make up the divisional reserve. An advanced seizure of the pier by First Lieutenant Hawkin's Scout-Sniper Platoon would precede the main assault.

Gen. Smith scheduled a large-scale amphibious exercise in Hawkes Bay on November 1. He planned for New Zealand trucks to haul the men back to Wellington at the end for a large dance. The entire 2nd Marine Division boarded the sixteen amphibious ships for the routine exercise. It was all a ruse. The ships weighed anchor and headed north to begin Operation Galvanic.

Task Force 53 assembled in New Hebrides on November 7. Adm. Hill arrived onboard the *Maryland*. Now that the Marines were keenly aware and operations were underway, they were more interested in the fourteen new Sherman tanks on board the *Ashland*. The 2nd Marine Division had never operated with medium tanks before. The rehearsal landings did little to prepare the Marines for the assault on Betio. Fleet carriers and air wings were assaulting other targets in the Solomons. Sherman tanks had nowhere to offload: the new LVT-2s were still somewhere to the north, underway for Tarawa. And naval gunships were bombarding Erradaka Island, away from the troops landing at Mele Bay.

One positive aspect of the amphibious assault rehearsal was that the Marines could practice embarking on rubber rafts. In the prewar Fleet Marine Force, the first battalion in each regiment was designated the Rubber Boat Battalion. This common site of a mini-flotilla inspired catcalls from other Marines. The main contentious issue during the post-rehearsal critique was the naval gunfire plan. The target island would receive the greatest concentration of naval gunfire in the war to date. Adm. Turner was optimistic about the outcome; he made his plans clear that they did not intend to just neutralize or destroy the island—but obliterate it. Gen. Smith reminded the senior naval officers that the Marines crossed the beach with bayonets. Their only armor would be khaki shirts.

While on New Hebrides, Colonel Marshall, the commander of

Combat Team Two became too ill to continue. Gen. Smith promoted Col. Shoup to relieve Col. Marshall. Shoup knew the 2nd Marines, and he knew the plan. The architect was now the executor.

Once underway, Adm. Hill ordered the various commanders of Task Force 53 to brief troops on the destination and mission. Tarawa was a surprise to most of the men. Many had believed they were heading for Wake Island. On the day before D-Day, Gen. Smith sent a message to the 2nd Division officers and men. In his message, he reassured his men that the Navy would stay and provide support throughout the campaign—unlike in the Guadalcanal Campaign. The troops attentively listened to these words coming over the loudspeakers:

We are embarked on a great offensive to destroy the enemy in the Central Pacific. The Navy will screen our operation and support our attack tomorrow with the greatest concentration of naval gunfire and aerial bombardment in the history of war. The Navy will remain with us until our objective has been secured. Garrison troops are already en route to relieve us as soon as we have completed our work. Good luck and God bless you all.

As the sun set on Task Force 53 on the evening of D -1, it seemed strategic surprise had been attained. More good news came with the report that small convoys of LSTs transporting the LVT-2s arrived safely from Samoa and had joined the formation. All the pieces were coming together.

D-DAY AT BETIO

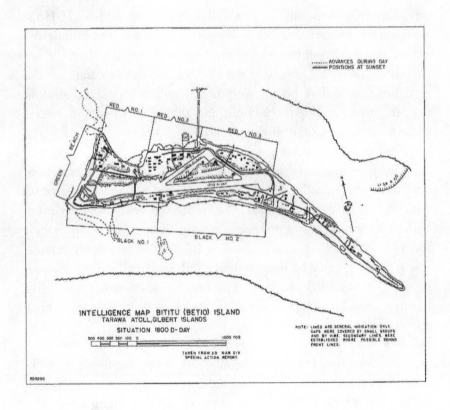

INTELLIGENCE MAP BITITU (BETIO) ISLAND
TARAWA ATOLL, GILBERT ISLANDS

SITUATION 1800 D-DAY

SHORTLY AFTER MIDNIGHT ON D-DAY, the crowded transports of Task Force 53 arrived off Tarawa. The sailors cheered as the public address system played the Marine Hymn to the 2/2 Marines scrambling over the sides and down the cargo nets at 0320.

This was when things started to go wrong.

Adm. Hill, the amphibious task force commander, realized the transports were in the wrong anchorage. He directed the fire support ships to immediately shift to the correct site. While the landing craft bobbed away along in the wake of the ships, several Marines were halfway down the cargo nets when the ships unexpectedly weighed anchor. Choppy seas made matching the exact LVTs with their assigned assault teams dangerous in the darkness.

Few tactical plans survived the opening rounds of execution in this amphibious operation. The D-Day plan was for the H-Hour assault wave to start at 0830. A fast carrier strike would initiate the action with a thirty-minute bombing raid at 0545. After that, the fire support ships would bombard the island from a close range for the next two hours. The planes would then return for a final strafing run, five minutes before H-Hour, and then shift to inland targets while the Marine Corps stormed ashore.

None of this went according to plan.

The Japanese were alerted by the predawn activities offshore and initiated the battle. Their garrison opened fire on Task Force 53 with big naval guns at 0505. The *Maryland's* and *Colorado's* main batteries returned fire at once, and several 16-inch shells found their mark. A huge fireball signaled the destruction of an enemy ammunition bunker at one of the Japanese's gun positions. After other fire support ships joined in, Adm. Hill ordered a cease-fire thirty-five minutes later. He'd expected the air attack to begin. A long silence and no air assault.

The carrier air group changed plans. They postponed the strike by thirty minutes. Their modifications were never relayed to Adm. Hill. Hill's problems were aggravated by the communication loss on his flagship after the ship's main battery's initial crushing salvo. The

Japanese coastal defense guns were damaged, but still dangerous. This mistake gave the Japanese almost thirty minutes to adjust and recover. Adm. Hill was frustrated at every turn and ordered his ships to resume firing at 0605. At 0610, carrier fast attack planes appeared. They bombed and strafed the island for the next few minutes. Throughout this confusion, the sun rose into a macabre background of thick, black smoke.

The destroyers, cruisers, and battleships of Task Force 53 bombarded Betio for the next few hours. The shock and awe of the shelling was a vivid experience for the Marines. A combat photographer, Staff Sergeant Hatch, recalled:

We really didn't see how we could do anything but just go in there and bury the Japanese. This wasn't even going to be a fight. Surely no mortal man could live through this destroying power. Any Japs on the island would have to be dead by now.

SSgt. Hatch was proved wrong by a geyser of water fifty yards to the starboard side of his ship. The Japanese resumed fire and targeted the vulnerable troop transports underway for the second time that morning.

Gen. Smith and Adm. Hill onboard *Maryland* struggled to get information throughout the long day. Their best source of information was from a Kingfisher observation aircraft, launched by the battleships. Adm. Hill asked the pilot if the reef was covered with water and received a negative answer. The first wave of LVTs, with over seven hundred embarked Marines, left the assembly area and headed toward the departure line.

The embarked Marines in the LVTs had a difficult, long morning. Cross deck transfers were dangerous in choppy seas while 8-inch shells exploded around them. They began a long run to the beach—ten miles away. The LVTs started on time but fell behind schedule quickly. The LVT-1s of the first wave failed to maintain the 4-knot speed of advance due to a strong westerly current. This, combined with the weight of the improvised armor plating, reduced the buoyancy. A psychological factor was also at work. Col. Edson had criticized the LVT crews for landing five minutes early during the rehearsal. He had made it clear that early arrival was inexcusable and preferred a late arrival. The three struggling columns of LVTs would not make the beach by the intended hour of 0830. This caused H-Hour to be postponed twice to 0900. All hands did not receive this information.

Two destroyers, *Dashiell* and *Ringgold,* entered the lagoon, following the minesweepers to provide close fire support. Once in the lagoon, the minesweeper *Pursuit* became the primary control ship and directly took a position on the departure line. The *Pursuit* turned her searchlights seaward and provided the LVTs with a beacon of light through the thick smoke and dust. At 0825, as the first wave of LVTs crossed the line, they were still 6,000 yards away from the target beaches.

Minutes after, carrier aircraft roared over Betio, right on time for the original H-Hour but unaware of the new times. Adm. Turner specifically provided all of the players in Operation Galvanic with this warning:

Times to strafe the beaches regarding H-Hour approximate. The distance of the boat from the beach will be a governing factor.

Adm. Hill called them off. The assault planes remained on station with depleted ammunition and fuel levels.

The LVTs chugged shoreward in three long waves. They were separated by 300-yard intervals. Wave One contained forty-two LVT-1s, followed by Wave Two with twenty-four LVT-2s, and Wave Three with twenty-one LVT-2s. Behind these tracked vehicles were Waves Four and Five of Higgins boats. Each of the assault battalion commanders were in Wave Four. Astern, the *Ashland* ballasted down and launched fourteen LCMs (or Landing Craft Mechanized), all carrying a medium Sherman tank. Four other LCMs trailed, transporting light tanks with 37mm guns.

Just before 0800, Col. Shoup and elements of his tactical command post debarked and headed to the line of departure. A bulky sergeant stood close to Col. Shoup and shielded the radio from the salt spray. Of all the communication failures and blackouts on D-Day, Col. Shoup's radio remained functional longer. It served him better than radios of any other commander—Japanese or American—on the island.

At 0854, Adm. Hill ordered a cease-fire, even though the assault waves were still 4,000 yards out from shore. Col. Edson and Gen. Smith objected. Still, Adm. Hill considered the enormous pillars of smoke unsafe for overhead fire support. After the bombing ceased, the LVTs made their final approach into the teeth of long-range machine-gun fire and artillery airbursts. The artillery could have been fatal to troops crowded into the open-topped LVTs, but the Japanese had loaded the projectiles with high explosives instead of steel shell fragments, which only doused the Marines with "hot sand." This was the last tactical mistake the Japanese made on D-Day.

The aborted airstrike returned at 0855 for five minutes of ineffective strafing along the beaches. The pilots followed their wrist-watches instead of the progress of the lead LVTs. Two naval landing boats started toward the end of the long pier at the reef's edge. 1stLt. Hawkins and his Scout Sniper Battalion with a squad of combat engineers charged out. They made quick work of Japanese gun placements along the pier with their flamethrowers and explosives.

The LVTs of Wave One struck the beach and crawled over the reef. These parts of Col. Shoup's plan were executed flawlessly. The bombardment, as extraordinary as it had been, failed to soften the Japanese defenses. Little of the ships' fire had been directed against the landing beaches.

Adm. Shibasaki vowed to defeat the amphibious assault units at the water's edge. The well-protected Japanese shook off the sand and manned their guns. The curbing of all naval gunfire for the first thirty minutes of the assault was a fateful mistake for Adm. Hill. This gave the Japanese time to shift their forces from the southern and western beaches to reinforce the northern positions. The Japanese defenders were stunned and groggy from the naval pounding and sight of the LVTs crossing the barrier reef. However, Adm. Shibasaki's killing zone was still intact. The Japanese met the amphibious assault waves with a steady volume of combined arms fire.

The first wave of LVTs approaching the final 200 yards of beaches Red One and Red Two were the most challenging. Well aimed fire from anti-boat, 40mm, and heavy and light machine guns hammered the Marines. The assault team fired back with their .50-caliber machine guns mounted on each of the LVT-1s, firing over 10,000 rounds. The exposed gunners were easy targets, and dozens were cut down. The LVT battalion commander, Maj. Drews—who worked with Shoup to make this assault possible—took over a machine gun from a fallen crewman and was killed instantly by a bullet through his eye. One of Maj. Drew's company commanders mentioned later he saw a Japanese officer standing defiantly on the seawall, waving his pistol, "just daring us to come ashore."

The LVTs pushed through. The touchdown times staggered at intervals of ten minutes on each beach. The first LVT to land was a vehicle nicknamed "My Deloris," driven by PFC Moore. My Deloris was the right guide vehicle on Red Beach One and hit the beach squarely on "the bird's beak." PFC Moore tried to drive his LVT over the 5-foot seawall, but the vehicle stalled in a vertical position while Japanese machine guns riddled troops inside. PFC Moore reached for his rifle and found it shot in half. He later recalled what happened next on the LVT:

The sergeant stood up and yelled, 'everybody out!' but as soon as the words left his mouth, machine-gun bullets ripped the top of his head off.

PFC Moore and a handful of others escaped the LVT and

destroyed two machine-gun positions a few yards away. All would either be killed or injured during the assault . Few of the LVTs could negotiate the 5-foot seawall. While the LVTs stalled on the beach, they were vulnerable to howitzer and mortar fire, as well as hand grenades thrown into the troop compartments by Japanese troops on the other side of the barrier.

One crew chief of the vehicle, Cpl. Spillane, a baseball prospect with the St. Louis Cardinals before the war, caught two Japanese grenades barehanded in midair and tossed them back over the wall. He caught a third grenade that exploded in his hand and fatally wounded him.

MAELSTROM ON BETIO

WAVES Two and Three of the LVT-2s were protected by a 3/8 inch boilerplate hastily installed in Samoa. These waves suffered even more intense fire. The large-caliber anti-boat Japanese guns destroyed several of the LVT-2s.

Machine gunner PFC Baird, aboard one of the embattled LVTs, recounted what he saw:

After we were 100 yards in, the enemy fire was awful damn intense and only getting worse. They were knocking us out left and right. A tractor would get hit, stop, and burst into flames. Men jumped out like torches.

PFC Baird's LVT was hit by a shell and killed many of the troops. He recalled:

I grabbed my carbine and an ammunition box. I stepped over a couple fellas lying there dead and put my hand on the side to roll over into the

water. I didn't want to put my head up. The bullets poured over us like a
sheet of rain.

The LVTs executed the assault according to Gen. Smith's expectations. Eight out of the eighty-seven vehicles in the first three waves were lost in the assault. Fifteen others were so damaged and riddled with holes that they sank when reaching deep water while seeking to shuttle more troops to shore. Within ten minutes, the LVTs landed over 1,500 Marines on Betio's north shore. While a brilliant start to the operation, the problem was sustaining the momentum of the assault. The neap tide predictions were accurate. No landing craft could cross that reef on D-Day.

Col. Shoup hoped that enough LVTs would survive to permit a wholesale transfer operation with the boats along the edge of the reef. It would not work. The LVTs suffered more casualties. Several vehicles, afloat for only five hours, ran out of gas. Others needed to be used immediately for the evacuation of wounded Marines. The already flawed communications deteriorated even more as the radio sets suffered water damage from enemy fire. The surviving LVTs continued on. But after 1015, most troops had waded ashore from the reef, crossing distances of 1,000 yards, under well-aimed fire. The Marines of the 3/2 were walloped on Red Beach One. Company K suffered casualties from the stronghold on the left. Company I crossed the seawall but paid a high price—losing their company commander before he could even debark from his LVT. Both units lost more than half of their men within the first two hours.

Major Michael Ryan's Company L was forced to wade ashore when their boats grounded on the reef, taking over 35% casualties. Maj. Ryan spotted one lone trooper through the fire and smoke scrambling over a parapet on the beach to the right, marking a new landing point. When Company L finally reached the shore, Maj. Ryan looked back over his shoulder, and all he could see were heads with rifles held over them. He ordered his men to make as small of a target as possible. Ryan assembled the various stragglers in a sheltered area along Green Beach.

In the fourth wave, Major Schoettel remained in his boat with the remnants of his Marines. He was convinced that his landing team had been destroyed beyond relief. He had no contact with Major Ryan. Schoettel received fragmented reports that seventeen of his thirty-seven officers were combat ineffective casualties.

In the center, the 2/2 Marines were thumped hard coming ashore. The Japanese strong point in the re-entrant between the two beaches created turmoil among the Marines scrambling over the sides of their stalled and beached LVTs. Five out of six of Company E's officers were killed. Company F took 50% casualties getting ashore and negotiating the seawall to seize a foothold. Company G barely clung to a crowded stretch of beach along the seawall in the middle. Two infantry platoons and two machine gun platoons were driven away from their beach. They were forced to land on Red Beach One, joining "Major Ryan's orphans."

When Lieutenant Colonel Amey's boat ran against the reef, he hailed a passing LVTs for a transfer. After that, LtCol. Amey's LVT became hung up on a barbed wire obstacle several hundred yards off Red Beach Two. Amey drew his pistol and shouted for his men to follow him into the water. As he got closer to the beach, LtCol. Amey turned to encourage his men:

Come on! These bastards can't beat us.

A machine gun fire burst hit him in the throat—killing him instantly. His XO, Major Rice, and another LVT landed far to the west behind Major Ryan. Lieutenant Colonel Walter Jordan was the senior officer present with the 2/2. He was one of the several observers from the 4th Marine Division, and only one of a handful of survivors from LtCol. Amey's LVT.

LtCol. Jordan did what any Marine would do under the circumstances: he took command. Jordan tried to rebuild the pieces of the landing team into a cohesive fighting force.

The only amphibious assault unit that got ashore without significant casualties was the 2/8 on Red Beach Three, east of the pier. This good fortune was attributed to the continued direct fire support the 2/8 received, throughout its run to the beach, from the two destroyers in the lagoon. The fire support from the two ships provided a preliminary fire from such a short-range. It kept the Japanese defenders on the island's eastern edge buttoned up. As a result, the 2/8 only suffered less than 25% casualties in the first three LVT waves. Company E made a significant penetration by crossing the barricade and the taxiway. Still, five of its six officers were shot down in the first ten minutes ashore. The 2/8 was fighting against one of the most sophisticated defensive positions on the islands. These fortifications to their left flank would keep the Marines boxed in for the next forty-eight hours.

Major "Jim" Crowe was the commander of the 2/8 Marines. A former enlisted man, gunner, distinguished rifleman, and star football player, he was a tower of strength through the battle. He carried a combat shotgun cradled in his arm. With his trademark red mustache, he exuded professionalism and confidence that were sorely needed on Betio that day. Maj. Crowe ordered the coxswain of his Higgins boat to "put the god damn boat in." The Higgins boat hit the reef at high speed, sending Marines sprawling. Crowe quickly recovered and ordered his men over the sides and then led them through hundreds of yards of shallow water. They reached the shore intact only four minutes behind the last wave of LVTs.

Crowe was accompanied by a combat photographer who recalled the major clenching a cigar in his teeth and standing upright, growling at his men:

Look, these sons of bitches can't hit me. Why do you think they can hit you? Get your asses moving. Go!

Red Beach Three was in capable hands.

By 0945 on Betio, Maj. Crowe was well-established, with a penetration to the airfield. A distinct gap existed between the 2/8 and the survivors of 2/2 in small clusters along Red Beach Two under LtCol. Jordan's command. It was a dangerous gap because of the Japanese fortifications between Beaches One and Two. Only a few members of 3/2 on the left flank and a growing collection of Marines under Maj. Ryan were on Green Beach.

Major Schoettel was floating beyond the reef. Col. Shoup was likewise in a Higgins boat, but starting his move toward the beach. Other Marines waded ashore under increasing enemy fire. The tanks were forced to unload from the LCMs at the reef's edge, searching for recon teams to lead them ashore.

Communications were a nightmare. The TBX radios of Crowe, Shoup, and Schoettel were still operational. But there was either dead silence or complete havoc on the command nets. No one on the flagship knew of Maj. Ryan's successful debark on the western end, or of LtCol. Amey's death and LtCol. Jordan's assumption of command. An early report from an unknown source flashed over the command nets:

Have landed. Unusually heavy opposition. Casualties 70%. Can't hold.

Col. Shoup ordered the 1/2 regimental reserve to land on Red Beach Two and work west. This would take time because the men were still awaiting orders at the line of departure, but all were waiting embarked in boats. Col. Shoup assembled enough LVTs to transport companies A and B. The 3rd Infantry Company and the Weapons Company had yet to wade ashore through this chaotic assault. Most of the LVTs were destroyed en route by anti-boat guns. Japanese gunners now had the range down pat. Five vehicles were driven away by the intense fire and landed west at Maj. Ryan's position, giving him another 113 troops to add to Green Beach.

The rest of companies A and B stormed ashore and penetrated

several hundred feet, expanding the perimeter. Other troops sought refuge along the pier and tried to commandeer a passing LVT. Many of the regimental reserve 1/2 troops did not complete the landing until the following morning. It was typical for an LVT driver and his gunners to be shot down by enemy machine gun fire. The surviving crewmen would get the stranded vehicle started again, but only in reverse. The vehicle would back wildly through the entire impact zone before breaking down again, causing several men to not reach the shore until sunset.

Naval commanders received their first clear signal that things were going wrong on the beach when a derelict LVT chugged astern with no one at the controls. They dispatched a boat to retrieve the vehicle and discovered three dead Marines aboard the LVT. Their bodies were brought on board and buried with full honors at sea. These were the first of hundreds of men consigned to the deep because of the maelstrom on Betio.

After the communications were restored on the *Maryland,* Gen. Smith tried to make sense of the conflicting and intermittent messages coming in through the ship's command net. At 1036 Gen. Smith reported to the V Amphibious Corps:

Successful landing on beaches Red Two and Three. Toehold on Red One. And committing one LT from division reserved. Still encountering strong resistance.

Col. Shoup was trying to navigate getting ashore. When his Higgins boat was stopped at the reef, he transferred into a passing LVT. He joined Colonel Evans Carlson, a legend for his exploits on Guadalcanal and Makin. He took command of the 1/10 Artillery detachment. Their LVT made three attempts to land—each time the enemy fire was too intense. On the third attempt, the vehicle was hit and disabled. Col. Shoup took a painful shell fragment wound in his leg but led his men out of the LVT and into the fight. He stood in waist-deep water surrounded by thousands of dead fish and floating bodies. Shoup manned his radio and tried desperately to get organized combat units ashore to sway the fight's balance.

Col. Shoup had hoped that the Sherman tanks could break the gridlock. This was the combat debut of the Marine Corps' medium tanks but was discouraging on D-Day. The 2nd Marine Division did not understand how to employ tanks against fortified positions. When four Shermans reached Red Beach Three, later in the morning, Maj. Crowe waved them forward with orders to knock out all enemy positions. The tank crews, who were buttoned up under fire, were practically blind in their tanks. With no accompanying infantry, they were destroyed one by one. Some were knocked out by the Japanese 75mm guns, while others were damaged by friendly fire from American dive bombers.

Six other Shermans that tried to land on Red Beach One were preceded by a dismounted guide to warn off underwater shell craters. These guides were shot down every few minutes by Japanese marksmen. Each time, another volunteer would step forward to continue the movement. Combat engineers had blown a hole in the seawall for the tanks to pass through, but the way was blocked with wounded and dead Marines. Rather than run over their fellow Marines, the tank commander reversed his column and went around toward a second opening blasted in the seawall.

While the Shermans operated in murky, chaotic waters, four tanks foundered in shell holes on the detour. Inland on the beach, one of the surviving Sherman's engaged a Japanese light tank. The medium American tank demolished its small opponent, but not before the doomed Japanese tank released one final 37mm round—a phenomenal shot—right down the barrel of the Sherman.

RED BEACH TWO

BY THE END of the day, only two of the fourteen Sherman tanks were still operational. Maintenance crews worked desperately to retrieve a third tank, *Cecilia*, on Green Beach for Maj. Ryan. Japanese gunners sank all four of the LCMs transporting the light tanks into the battle before the boats even reached the reef. The tank battalion commander, Colonel Swenceski, was assumed killed in action while wading ashore. He was severely wounded but survived by crawling on top of a pile of dead bodies to keep from drowning until he was discovered the next day.

Col. Shoup sent a message to the flagship at 1045 on D-Day voicing his frustration:

Our tanks no good. Stiff resistance, need half-tracks.

The regimental weapons company's half-tracks with their 75mm guns fared no better getting ashore than any other combat units that morning. One half-track was sunk in its LCM transport by long-range artillery fire before reaching the reef. A second half-track ran the entire gauntlet but got stuck in the loose sand at the water's edge and was destroyed. The situation was now critical.

Individual courage and initiative inspired the scattered remnants throughout the chaos along the exposed beachhead. Staff Sergeant Bordelon was a combat engineer attached to the 2/2. After a Japanese shell disabled his LVT and killed most of the troops en route to the beach, Bordelon rallied the survivors and led them ashore on Red Beach Two. He stopped only long enough to prepare explosive charges. He knocked out two Japanese positions that had been firing on the assault waves. After attacking a third emplacement, he was hit by machine-gun fire but refused medical help and continued fighting. SSgt. Bordelon bolted back into the water and rescued a wounded Marine calling for help. As more intense fire opened up from another enemy position, Bordelon prepared one final demolition package and charged the Japanese gun position in a frontal assault. This is where his luck ran out. He was shot and killed. He later became the first of four men in the 2nd Marine Division to be awarded the Medal of Honor.

In another instance, Sgt. Roy Johnson single-handedly attacked a Japanese tank. He scrambled to the turret and dropped a grenade inside while sitting on the hatch, waiting for the detonation. Sgt. Johnson survived this but was later killed in the fighting on Betio. In the seventy-six hour battle, he was one of the 217 Marine sergeants to be wounded or killed.

A captain on Red Beach Three, who was shot through both arms and legs, sent a message to Maj. Crowe apologizing for letting him down.

Maj. Ryan later recalled a wounded Sgt., who he'd never seen before, limping up to him and asking where he was needed most.

PFC Moore, who was earlier disarmed and wounded, trying to drive "My Dolores" over the seawall, carried ammo to the machine gun crews for the rest of the day until he was evacuated to one of the transports.

Other brave Marines retrieved a pair of 37mm antitank guns from a sunken landing craft. They manhandled them across several hundred yards under terrifying enemy fire. They dragged them across the beach to the seawall. While two Japanese tanks approached the beachheads, the Marines lifted the 900-pound anti-tank guns on top of the seawall. They calmly loaded, aimed, and fired. Knocking out one of the Japanese tanks at close range and chasing off the other.

Robert Sherrod was an experienced war correspondent for *Time* magazine. The landing on D-Day at Betio was the most frightening experience of his life. Sherrod accompanied Marines from the fourth wave of 2/2 and tried to wade ashore on Red Beach Two. In his own words:

No sooner did we hit the water than the Japanese machine guns really opened up on us. It was so painfully slow, we waded in such deep water.

We had 700 yards to walk slowly into direct machine-gun fire, looming into larger targets as we rose onto the higher ground. I was so scared, more than I'd ever been before. Those who weren't hit would always remember how the machine-gun bullets hissed into the water, inches to the right, inches to the left.

Col. Shoup moved toward the beach parallel to the pier. He ordered Major Ruud's 3/8 Marines to land on Red Beach Three—east of the pier. There were now no organized LVT units to transport the reserve battalion to the fight. Maj. Ruud was ordered to approach as near as he could to the landing boats and then wade the remaining distance into shore. Ruud received his orders from Col. Shoup at 1104. While the two officers were never more than a mile apart from each other for the next six hours, they could not communicate.

Maj. Ruud divided his landing team into seven waves. Once the boats approached, the reef confusion began. The Japanese zeroed their anti-boat guns on the landing craft with fearsome accuracy. They scored several direct hits as the bow ramp dropped. A distinct *clang* from an impacting shell would signal a split second before the explosion. SSgt. Hatch watching from the beach later recalled:

It happened at least a dozen times. The boat was blown completely out of the water and smashed bodies all over the place. I watched a Jap shell hit a landing craft directly that brought many Marines ashore. The explosion was horrific, and parts of the boat flew in all directions.

Navy coxswains watching the slaughter directly ahead stopped their boats seaward of the reef and ordered troops to debark. Many Marines loaded with extra ammunition or radios instantly sank into the deep water—many drowned. The reward for the troops whose coxswains made it into the reef was less sanguine. They waded through 600 yards of withering crossfire. Heavier, by far, than what the first assault waves experienced at H-Hour. The first wave slaughter of companies L and K was terrible. Over 70% fell while attempting to reach the beach.

Col. Shoup and his party frantically waved to groups of Marines to seek the pier's protection. While many did, several NCOs and officers had been hit, making the stragglers disorganized. The pier was a questionable shelter; it received sniper fire, and intermittent machine-gun fire from both sides. Col. Shoup was struck in nine places. A bullet came close to penetrating his bull-like neck. His runner crouching behind him was shot between the eyes by a Japanese sniper.

The commander of the 3/8 Weapons Company, Captain Carl Hoffman, fared no better getting ashore than the infantry companies ahead. His landing craft took a direct hit from a Japanese mortar, and he lost six or eight men right there. Capt. Hoffman's Marines veered toward the peer and then waded toward shore. Maj. Ruud was unable to contact Col. Shoup. And instead radioed his regimental commander, Colonel Elmer Hall:

Third wave landed on Red Beach Three. Practically wiped out. Fourth wave landed but only a few Marines ashore.

Col. Hall was in a small boat near the line of departure, unable to respond. General Hermle, Assistant Division Commander, intervened with this message:

Stay where you are or retreat out of gun range.

This only added to the confusion. Maj. Ruud did not reach the pier until late afternoon. At 1730 he was able to lead what was left of his men ashore.

Many Marines did not straggle in until the following day. Col.

Shoup dispatched what was left of the 3/8 to support Maj. Crowe's besieged 2/8. Other Marines were used to plug the gap between the 2/8 and the combined troops of the 2/2 and the 1/2.

When Col. Shoup finally reached Betio and established his command post. He was fifty yards in from the pier along the blind-side of a Japanese occupied bunker. Shoup posted guards to keep the enemy from launching any attacks. Still, the site's approaches were exposed, just like any other place on the flat island. Over twenty messengers were shot while bearing dispatches to and from Col. Shoup.

Combat photographer Sherrod crawled to look out at the exposed water on both sides of the pier. He counted over fifty disabled LVTs, boats, and tanks.

Col. Shoup admitted to him, "We need more men. We're in a tight spot." The situation did not look good.

Col. Shoup's first order of business after reaching dry ground was to seek updated reports from his landing team commanders. Tactical communications were worse now than they had been during the morning assault. Col. Shoup still had no contact with any troops on Red Beach One, nor could he raise Gen. Smith on *Maryland*. A messenger arrived with a report from 2/2:

All communications out except runners. We need help. Situation bad. CO killed. No word from E Company.

Col. Shoup found LtCol. Jordan and ordered him to take command of the 2/2. Shoup reinforced him with elements of the 1/2 and 3/8. He gave Jordan an hour to organize and rearm the assorted attachments. Shoup then ordered him to proceed inland to attack the airstrip and expand the beachhead. Col. Shoup then ordered Col. Carlson to hitch a ride to the *Maryland* and inform Gen. Smith of the situation personally. He told Col. Carlson to tell the general, "We're going to stick it out and fight."

Carlson departed immediately. But because of the hazards and confusion between the line of departure and the beach, he did not reach the flagship with his message until 1800.

FOG OF WAR

Col. Shoup focused his attention on the critical matters of resupply. Beyond the pier were over a hundred small craft that circled aimlessly. They carried assorted supplies from cargo and transport ships. They unloaded as quickly as they could in compliance with Adm. Nimitz's orders of "Get the hell in and then get the hell out."

The unorganized unloading hindered the fight ashore. Shoup was not sure of which boat held what supplies. He sent word that only the most critical supplies were to be sent to the pier: LVT fuel, ammunition, water, blood plasma, and more radios. The naval gunfire support since the landing was terrific, but it was time for the Marines to bring their own artillery to the beachhead. The original plan of landing the 1/10 Marines at Red Beach One was no longer practical.

Shoup conferred with Lieutenant Colonel Presley Rixey and agreed to land on Red Beach Two's left flank with the 75mm howitzers. These expeditionary guns would be broken down and manhandled ashore. LtCol. Rixey had seen close up what happened when the 3/8 tried to wade ashore from the reef. He went after the last few LVTs. There were only enough operational vehicles for two sections of Batteries A and B. In the confusion, three Battery C sections followed the LVTs toward the shore in their open boats. Luck smiled on the artillerymen. The LVTs landed with intact guns in the late afternoon. When the trailing boats were hung up on the reef, Marines dragged the heavy components through the bullet swept waters to the pier and made it ashore by twilight. There was now close-in fire support available at dawn.

Gen. Julian Smith knew little of what was happening. He continued trying to piece together the tactical situation onshore. Smith received reports from staff officers afloat and in float planes. He decided the situation in the early afternoon was in desperate straits.

Although he had elements of five infantry battalions ashore, their toehold was unstable. Gen. Smith decided the gap between Red Beach One and Red Beach Two had not been closed. And that the left flank on Red Beach Three was not secure. Smith assumed that Col. Shoup was still alive and in command, but he could not afford to gamble. Over the next few hours, the commanding general did his best to influence all-action ashore from the flagship. Smith's first step was to send a radio message to Gen. Holland Smith. He requested the use of the 6th Marines to division control because the situation was in doubt. He also ordered his last remaining landing team, 1/8 Marines, to the line of departure. Gen. Julian Smith reorganized another emergency division composed of engineers, artillery, and service troop units.

Gen. Julian Smith ordered Gen. Hermle to proceed to the end of the pier and assess the situation and report back. Hermle took his small staff and promptly debarked from the *Monrovia* headed toward the smoking island—but the trip took four hours. During this time, Gen. Julian Smith received a message from Maj. Schoettel, still afloat seaward at the reef:

Command post located on back of Red Beach One. Situation as before.
Lost all contact with assault elements.

Gen. Smith replied:

Land at any cost. Regain control of your battalion and continue to attack.

Maj. Schoettel reached the beach at sunset. It was well into the next day before he could work west and consolidate the scattered Marines. Gen. Smith received authorization to take control of the 6th Marines at 1525. Smith now had four battalions of landing teams available at his disposal. The question was how to feed them into the fight without getting them annihilated like Maj. Ruud's experience trying to land the 3/8.

Again, Gen. Smith's communications failed him. At 1740 he received a message from Hermle that he had reached the pier and was under fire. Ten minutes later, Smith ordered Hermle to take command of all forces onshore. Hermle never received these orders. Gen. Smith did not know his message failed to get through, and Hermle remained at the pier sending runners to Col. Shoup, who told him to "Get the hell out from underneath that pier." They tried with little success to unscrew the two-way movement of casualties and supplies to shore.

Throughout the long day, Col. Hall and his staff languished in their Higgins boats next to the 1/8 waiting at the line of departure. They were wet, cramped, hungry, and tired with many seasick Marines. Later in the afternoon, Gen. Smith ordered Hall to land all of his remaining units on the beach on the northeast tip of the island and work west toward Col. Shoup's ragged lines. This was extremely risky. Gen. Smith's primary concern was that the Japanese would counterattack from the eastern tail of the island against his left flank. Once he had the 6th Marines, Gen. Smith later admitted he would've sacrificed a battalion landing team if it meant saving the landing force from being overrun by a Japanese counterattack during the night.

Luckily, Hall never received this message from Gen. Smith.

Later that afternoon, a float plane reported to Smith that a unit crossed the departure line and headed for the left flank of Red Beach Two. Gen. Smith assumed it was Hall going to the wrong beach. But this was the beginning of Rixey's artillerymen moving ashore. The 8th Marines spent the night in their boats waiting for orders. Gen. Smith did not discover this until early the next morning.

On Betio, Maj. Ryan reported to Col. Shoup that several hundred Marines and two tanks had penetrated over 500 yards beyond Red Beach One on the island's western end. This was now the most successful progress of the day and welcome news to Col. Shoup, because he'd feared the worst. He'd assumed Schoettel's companies and all other strays who'd veered in that direction were wiped out. This was more news that Col. Shoup could not convey to Gen. Smith.

Maj. Ryan's troops were effective on the western end. They learned how to best operate the medium tanks and carved out a substantial beachhead. They overran several Japanese pillboxes and turrets. Aside from the tanks, Maj. Ryan's men had only infantry weapons. They had no demolitions or flamethrowers. Maj. Ryan new from his earlier experiences fighting in the Solomons that positions reduced by only grenades could come alive again. He decided by late afternoon to pull back his thin lines and consolidate. In his words:

I was convinced that without any flamethrowers or explosives to clean them out, we needed to pull back . . . to a perimeter that could be defended against a counterattack by Japanese troops still hidden in the bunkers.

The fundamental choice by Marines on Betio was whether to stay put on the beach or try and crawl over the seawall to fight inland. Much of the day, the fire came across the coconut logs so intensely that a man could lift his hand and get it shot off. Late on

D-Day, many Marines were too demoralized to advance. Major Ravoth Tompkins brought messages from Gen. Hermle to Col. Shoup. Tompkins arrived on Red Beach Two at the foot of the pier at dusk on D-Day. He was appalled at the sight of so many Marine stragglers. Tompkins wondered why the Japanese didn't just use mortars on the first night. He later reported that Marines lying on the beach were so thick you couldn't walk through them.

The conditions on Red Beach One were congested as well, but there was a difference. Maj. Crowe was everywhere, "as cool as icebox lettuce." There weren't any stragglers. Maj. Crowe fed small groups of Marines into the lines, reinforcing his precarious hold on the left flank. Capt. Hoffman of the 3/8 Marines welcomed the integration of Crowe's 2/8 Marines. Hoffman needed help as darkness fell. He recalled:

There we were, toes in the water, casualties everywhere, dead and wounded all around us. But finally, a few Marines started to inch forward, a yard here, a yard there.

It was enough, Hoffman could see well enough to call in naval gunfire support. His men dug in for the night. To the west of Maj. Crowe's lines, and inland from Col. Shoup's command post, was Company B of the 1/2. They had settled in for the expected counterattack. Scattered in the bloody landing at midday, Company B had men from 12 to 14 different units, including sailors, who swam ashore from sinking boats. These men were all well-armed and no longer stragglers.

Of the 5,000 Marines that stormed the beaches of Betio on D-Day, 1,500 of them were missing, dead, or wounded by nightfall. The survivors held only a quarter of a square mile of coral and sand. Col. Shoup later described the location of his beachhead lines the night of D-Day as "a stock market graph." The Marines went to ground in the best fighting positions they could secure, whether in inland shell holes or along the splintered seawall. Despite the defensive positions and scrambled units, the fire discipline of the Marines was superb. The troops shared a grim confidence. They'd already faced the worst in getting ashore. They were ready for any *banzai* charges in the dark.

Gen. Smith on the *Maryland* was concerned. He recalled:

This was the crisis of the battle. Three-fourths of the island was in enemy hands. A concerted Japanese counterattack would've driven us into the sea.

Smith reported up his chain of command to Admirals Spruance, Turner, and Nimitz that the issue still remained in doubt. Adm. Spruance's staff began drafting plans for an emergency evacuation of the landing force.

Throughout the night of D-Day, the main struggle was Shoup and Hermle's attempt to try and advise Gen. Smith of the best place to land the reserves the following morning. Gen. Smith was astonished to learn at 0200, that Col. Hall was not ashore but still at the line of departure awaiting orders. Smith again ordered combat team eight to land on the eastern tip of the island at 0900 on D+1.

Gen. Hermle finally caught a boat back to one of the destroyers. He relayed Shoup's request to land reinforcements on Red Beach Two. Gen. Smith modified Col. Hall's orders. Smith ordered Hermle back to the flagship, irked at his assistant for not getting ashore and taking command. In the end, Gen. Hermle had done Smith a useful service by relaying the advice from Col. Shoup. As much as the 8th Marines would bleed in the next morning's assault, a landing on the island's eastern end would have been a disaster. Reconnaissance after the battle discovered those beaches to be the most intensely mined on the entire island.

D+1 AT BETIO

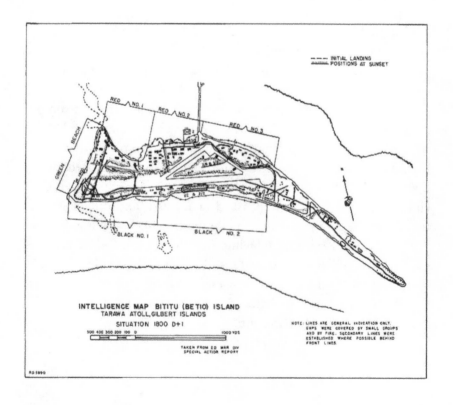

INTELLIGENCE MAP BITITU (BETIO) ISLAND
TARAWA ATOLL, GILBERT ISLANDS

SITUATION 1800 D+1

TAKEN FROM 2D MAR DIV
SPECIAL ACTION REPORT

THE TACTICAL SITUATION on Betio was perilous for most of the second day. During the morning, the Marines paid in blood for every attempt to land reserves or advance the ragged beachheads. Tarawa's beaches were gruesome and filled with the dead and dying. Col. Shoup surveyed the beach at first light and was horrified. In his own words:

It was a dreadful sight, bodies drifted slowly in the water just off the beach. The stench of dead bodies covered the island like a cloud.

The smell wafted out a bad omen to the line of departure for the 1/8 Marines getting ready to start their run into the beach. With an imperfect knowledge of the scattered forces and his faulty communications, Col. Shoup ordered each landing team commander to attack. LtCol. Jordan would take the south coast. Rudd and Crowe were to reduce the Japanese strongholds to their left and front. Maj. Ryan was to take all of Green Beach.

Col. Shoup's predawn request to Gen. Smith relayed a specific landing of the 1/8 on Red Beach Two close to the pier. Unfortunately, this critical component of Col. Shoup's request did not survive the communications route to Gen. Smith. The commanding general ordered Major Lawrence C. Hays Jr. and Col. Hall to land on Red Beach Two at 0615. Hays and Hall were oblivious of the situation ashore and assumed that the 1/8 would make a covered landing.

The Marines of the 1/8 had spent eighteen hours in the embarked Higgins boats, making endless circles through the night. The troops cheered when the boats finally made their turn toward the beach.

Things went wrong quickly. The tides failed to provide enough water for the boats to cross the reef. Hays' men debarked over the obstacle and started the 500-yard trek to shore. Dangerously far to the right flank and within the zone of Japanese guns firing from the strong re-entrant point. They were in the worst place they could be.

Japanese gunners began an unrelenting fire. Japanese snipers raked the Marines from the disabled LVTs they had infiltrated during the night. Multiple machine guns opened up on the waiting troops from every beached interisland schooner at the reef's edge. Hays' men fell at every turn.

The Marines tried to stop the slaughter. Col. Shoup called for naval gunfire support. Two 75mm howitzers protected by a sand berm, erected from a Seabee bulldozer, fired at the blockhouses at the Red Beach One/Two border using delayed fuses in high explosive shells. A squadron of F4F Wildcats attacked the Japanese defenders with machine guns and bombs. While these measures helped, the Japanese had caught the Marines in a withering crossfire.

Correspondent Sherrod watched this bloodbath in horror. In an hour, Sherrod counted at least two hundred bodies that did not move on the dry flats. He recalled:

One boat blows up, then another. The survivors start to swim for shore, but machine-gun bullets dot the water all around them. Far worse today than yesterday.

First Lieutenant Dean Ladd jumped into the water from his boat and was shot in the stomach. He recalled the troops' strict orders to not stop for the wounded and expected to die on the spot. One of his riflemen, PFC Sullivan, ignored the orders and saved his lieutenant's life. Ladd's rifle platoon suffered twenty-four casualties during the ship to shore assault.

First Lieutenant Frank Plant, the air liaison officer, was with Maj. Hays in the command Higgins boat. After the call, the craft slammed into the reef, Maj. Hays shouted for the men to debark. As he jumped in the water, the troops that followed him were cut down by the murderous fire. Lieut. Plant helped to pull the wounded back into the boat. He later wrote that the water all around him was colored purple with blood. As he hurriedly caught up with Maj. Hays, he was terrified at the sudden appearance of what he thought were Japanese fighters roaring toward him. But they were the Navy Wildcats screaming in to attack the Japanese. The pilots were excited but inconsistent. While one bomb hit the Japanese defenders, others missed by over 200 yards and contributed to the dying Marines' chaos. An angry Col. Shoup came on the radio:

Stop strafing. Bombs hitting our own troops.

It was only sheer courage of the survivors that got them ashore under such a hellish crossfire. Maj. Hays reported to Shoup at 0800 with only half of his landing team. He had taken over three hundred casualties while other men were missing and scattered along the beach and pier. His unit had lost all of its heavy weapons, demolitions, and flamethrowers. Col. Shoup directed Hays to attack west. Both men knew that small arms and courage would not overtake the Japanese in their fortified positions.

The combined forces of Majors Rudd in Crowe on Red Beach Three were full of fight and had sufficient weapons. Their left flank was flush against three large Japanese bunkers, each mutually supporting each other and unassailable. The stubby pier slightly to the east of the main pier turned into a bloody no-man's-land as the two sides fought for possession. Learning from the mistakes of D-Day, Maj. Crowe ensured his one surviving Sherman was always accompanied by infantry.

Rudd and Crowe benefited from the intense air support and naval gunfire on their left flank. Maj. Crowe was later to write that he was unimpressed with the aviators' effectiveness and accuracy, and that the aircraft never did that much good. But he was enthusiastic about the naval guns:

I had the three destroyers supporting me: the Ringgold, the Daschle, and the Anderson. Anything I asked for, I got. I authorized a direct fire from one of the destroyers in the lagoon at a command bunker only 50 yards ahead of us during the fight. They slammed the fire in there, and you could see arms and legs and everything just go up like that.

LtCol. Jordan managed to get some of his troops across the fire-swept airstrip inland from Red Beach Two all the way to the southern coast—making a significant penetration. Their toehold was precarious, and his Marines suffered heavy casualties. He recalled that he could not see the Japanese. Still, the fire came from every direction when Jordan lost contact with his lead elements. Col. Shoup ordered him across the island to reestablish command. Jordan did so at a significant hazard to himself. By the time his reinforcements arrived, LtCol. Jordan had only fifty men, who could be accounted for, from his landing team's 2/2 rifle companies. The colonel organized and supplied these men to the best of his abilities. Then, at Shoup's orders, he merged them with the reinforcements and stepped back into his original role as an observer.

SCOUT SNIPER PLATOON

THE HEROICS of the 2nd Marines Scout Sniper Platoon had been spectacular from the start, when they led the assault on the pier, just before H-Hour. 1stLt. Hawkins was an example of having a cool disregard for danger in every tactical situation.

While he displayed superhuman bravery, it would not protect him in the turmoil. A Japanese shell had wounded him on D-Day, and he shook off any attempts to treat his injuries. At dawn on D+1, he led his men in a series of attacks on Japanese strong points. Hawkins crawled up to a pillbox, fired his weapon point-blank through the gun ports, and threw grenades inside to finish the job. He was shot in the chest but continued to attack and took out three more pillboxes personally. Just after that, a Japanese shell tore him apart.

The division mourned his death, and he was awarded the Medal of Honor posthumously. Col. Shoup recalled:

It's not often that you can credit a first lieutenant with winning a battle, but Lieut. Hawkins came as near to it as any man possibly could have.

It was now up to Maj. Ryan and his makeshift battalion on the western side of Betio to make the most considerable contribution to winning the battle. Ryan's fortunes were enhanced by three developments during the night.

1. The Japanese did not counterattack his thin lines.
2. Seabees repaired his medium tank, *Cecilia*.
3. The arrival of a naval gunfire spotter, Lieutenant Thomas Green, with a fully functional radio.

Ryan organized a coordinated attack against the Japanese pillboxes, gun emplacements, and rifle pits concentrated on the island's southwestern corner. Slowed by communication failures, Ryan could talk to the fire support ships but not Col. Shoup. It took hours for his runners to negotiate the fire gauntlet and return with answers from Shoup's CP.

Ryan's first message to Shoup revealed his attack plans but was delayed because Col. Shoup called in an airstrike. After two more runners, the airstrike was canceled, and Ryan called in a naval gunfire strike on the southwest targets. Two of the destroyers in the lagoon responded accurately and promptly. Maj. Ryan launched a coordinated tank/infantry assault at 1120. In less than an hour, his makeshift force had seized all of Green Beach and was ready to move eastward toward the airfield and attack.

The communications were still awful. Maj. Ryan twice reported that the southern end of Green Beach was intensely mined. That message reached no higher headquarters. Gen. Smith on the *Maryland* did not receive any direct word of Maj. Ryan's successes. Smith was delighted when he learned he could land reinforcements on the covered beach and keep the unit integrity intact.

Gen. Smith conferred with Colonel Holmes, commander of the 6th Marines, as to the best way of getting the fresh combat teams into the fight. Due to the heavy casualties taken by Hays' battalion on Red Beach Two, Smith reassessed his landing on an unknown eastern end of the island. Maj. Ryan's good news quickly solved this problem. Smith ordered Holmes to land one of his battalions by rubber raft on Green Beach and have the second landing team boated in and prepared to wade ashore in support.

Gen. Smith received reports that the Japanese troops were retreating from the eastern end of Betio by wading across to the next islet: Bairiki. The Marines did not want to fight the same deadly enemy twice. Holmes ordered the 2/6 to land on Bairiki and "seal the back door." The 1/6 was ordered to land on Green Beach by rubber boat. The 3/6 was held in reserve and prepared to land at any assigned spot, probably Green Beach. Gen. Smith ordered the light tanks of Company B to land on Green Beach, supporting the 6th Marines.

These tactical plans took much longer to execute than envisioned. The 1/6 was waiting and ready to debark when their ship *Feland* was ordered underway because of a submarine threat. It would be hours before the *Feland* could return close enough to Betio and launch the rubber boats and the Higgins tow craft. These light tanks were now among the few critical items not loaded into the transports because they were in the very bottom of the cargo holds. During the first thirty-five hours of the landing, poor loading practices had further scrambled all supplies and equipment into intervening decks. It would take hours to clear the tanks and get them loaded on board.

Frustrated by the long delays, Shoup sent a message at 1345, asking for flamethrowers. He desperately wanted the 1/6 ashore to begin their attack. Col. Shoup, and his small staff were continually frustrated by logistical support problems. His team organized men to strip the dead of first-aid pouches, canteens, and ammunition. He also organized a shore party to create a false beachhead at the end of the pier.

The primary control officer onboard the minesweeper, *Pursuit*, Captain McGovern, eventually brought order by taking strict control of all unloading supplies. He used the surviving LVTs to keep the shuttle of casualties moving seaward and bring all critical items from the pier head to the beach.

This task was completed by men who hadn't slept in days and worked under constant enemy fire.

TIDE OF BATTLE

THE HANDLING of casualties was the most pressing logistical problem on D+1. The 2nd Marine Division was served heroically by its Navy corpsmen and doctors. Over ninety of these medical specialists were casualties in the onshore fighting.

Lieutenant Herman Brukhardt established an emergency room in a captured Japanese bunker. Some of the former occupants came to life, firing their rifles more than once. But, in over thirty-six hours and under brutal conditions, Lieut. Brukhardt treated 126 wounded men, only losing four.

The casualties were at first evacuated to the far off troopships. Because a long journey was so dangerous and wasteful of the few available LVTs or Higgins boats, the Marines began to deliver casualties to the destroyer *Ringgold* in the lagoon. Even though her sickbay had been destroyed by a 5-inch Japanese shell on D-Day, the destroyer still actively fired in support missions and accepted dozens of casualties.

Adm. Hill dispatched the troopship, *Doyen*, into the lagoon early on D+1 to be used as a primary critical receiving ship. Lieutenant Commander Oliver led a surgical team of five men with recent combat experience from the Aleutian Islands. In three days, Oliver's team treated over 550 wounded Marines. In his own words:

We'd run out of sodium pentathol and had to use ether. If a bomb would've hit us, Doyen would have blown off the face of the planet.

The Navy chaplains were also hard at work wherever the Marines were fighting onshore. They had heartbreaking work: administering last rites to the dying, consoling the wounded, and praying for the souls of the dead before the bulldozer came to cover the bodies from the unforgiving tropical sun.

The tide of battle now shifted toward the Americans by the middle of the afternoon on D+1. While the fighting was still intense, and Japanese fire deadly, the surviving Marines were now moving. No longer gridlocked in dangerous toeholds, LtCol. Rixey's howitzers made a new definition of close-in fire support. Supplies of fresh water and ammunition were improved. Morale was rising. The troops knew the 6th Marines would come in soon. LtCol. Rixey later wrote:

I thought up until 1300 today it was touch and go, after that I knew we would win.

Despair spread among the Japanese defenders. While they had shot down Marines at every turn they could—another would appear in his place: rifle blazing, well supported by naval and artillery guns. The great Japanese *Yogaki Plan* was a failure. Only a few enemy aircraft would attack the island every night. American transports were never seriously threatened, and the Japanese fleet never joined the battle. Japanese troops began to commit suicide rather than risk being captured.

Col. Shoup noticed the shift in momentum. Despite his frustration over the miscommunications and delays, he was in good spirits. He sent a situation report to Gen. Smith at 1600—with a famous last line:

Casualties: many. Percentage dead: unknown. Combat efficiency: We are winning.

At 1655, the 2/6 landed on Bairiki against light opposition. During the night, the 2/10 landed on the same island and began firing its howitzers. Rixey's fire direction center on Betio helped this process. The forward artillery observer, attached to Maj. Crowe's 2/8 on Red Beach One, adjusted the fire of the Bairiki guns he'd practiced on in New Zealand. Gen. Smith finally had artillery in place on Bairiki.

Meanwhile, the 1/6 were finally on the move. After a day of many false starts, the Marines prepared for their assault mission, which Gen. Smith had changed from the east end to Green Beach. When the *Feland* returned to within a reasonable range, the 1/6 Marines disembarked. They used the tactics developed with the Navy during the rehearsal on Efate. The men loaded onboard the Higgins boat's, which towed their rubber raft to the beach. The Marines embarked on board the rafts with up to ten troops per craft and began the 1,000-yard paddle toward Green Beach.

Major "Willie K." Jones, commander of the 1/6 Marines, later remarked that he did *not* feel like the "admiral of the condom fleet," as he helped paddle his raft shoreward. He noted that his battalion was spread out over the ocean from horizon to horizon. Maj. Jones was alarmed at the frequent appearance of anti-boat mines moored to the coral heads beneath the surface, endangering his 150 rubber rafts.

His rafts passed over the mines without incident. Jones also had two LVTs accompanying his ship to shore movement, each preloaded with rations, ammo, water, medical supplies, and spare radio equipment. While guided in by the rafts, one of the LVTs made it ashore, but the second drifted into a mine that blew the heavy vehicle ten feet in the air, killed most of the crew, and destroyed all of the supplies. It was a severe but not critical loss. The landing force suffered no other casualties coming ashore, thanks to Maj. Ryan's men. Jones' battalion was the first to land intact on Betio.

It was well after dark by the time Maj. Jones assumed his defensive positions behind Maj. Ryan's lines. The light tanks of Company B continued their attempt to come ashore on Green Beach. Because of the high surf and the distance between the reef, the beach hindered the landing effort. While a platoon of six tanks eventually reached the beach, the rest of the company moved its boats toward the pier and worked all night to get ashore onto Red Beach Two. The 3/6 Marines remained afloat in Higgins boats beyond the reef for an uncomfortable night.

That evening Col. Shoup turned to war correspondent Robert Sherrod and said:

We're winning, but the bastards have a lot of bullets left. I think we should clean it all up tomorrow.

After dark, Gen. Smith sent Col. Edson ashore to command all Betio and Bairiki forces. Col. Shoup had done a magnificent job, but it was now time for the senior colonel to take command. Edson had two artillery battalions and eight reinforced infantry battalions deployed on the two islands. The 3/6 Marines were scheduled to land early on D+2. Virtually all combat and support elements of the 2nd Marine Division would now be deployed.

Col. Edson found Shoup's command post at 2030. He greeted the barrel-chested warrior still on his feet, haggard and grimy but full of fight. Col. Edson took command and allowed Col. Shoup to concentrate on his own reinforced combat team, and they began making plans for the next morning.

Years later, Gen. Julian Smith looked back on the pivotal day of November 21, 1943, and wrote:

We were losing until we won. Many things went wrong, and the Japanese inflicted severe casualties on us, but from this point on, the issue was no longer in doubt at Tarawa.

D+2 AT BETIO

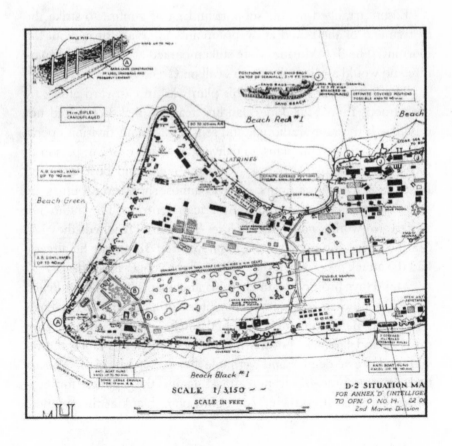

WAR CORRESPONDENT KEITH WHEELER from *the Chicago Daily News* sent this dispatch from Tarawa on D+2:

It looks like the Marines are winning on this blood-soaked, bomb-hammered, stinking little island.

Col. Edson's plan of attack on D+2 was to have the 1/6 Marines attack eastward along south beach and link up with the 1/2 and 2/2. He issued his attack orders at 0400 and attached the 1/8 to the 2nd Division Marines. They were to attack at daylight to the west along north beach and eliminate all Japanese resistance pockets between Red Beach One and Two. After that, the 1/8 would continue the attack east.

Edson arranged for air support and naval gunfire to strike the eastern end of the island at twenty-minute intervals throughout the morning. The 3/6 Marines were still embarked at the line of departure and would await Col. Shoup's call on Green Beach.

The key to the success of this plan was an eastward attack by fresh troops from Maj. Jones' landing team. Col. Edson could not raise the 1/6 on any radio net and sent his assistant division operations officer, Maj. Tompkins, to deliver the attack order in person to Jones. Maj. Tompkins' odyssey from the command post to Green Beach took over three hours. He was almost shot, several times, by Japanese snipers and nervous American sentries. The radio net started to work again just before Tompkins reached the 1/6 Marines. Maj. Jones later wrote he never told Tompkins he already had the attack order when the exhausted messenger arrived.

Maj. Hays promptly launched his attack at 0700 on Red Beach Two. He attacked westward on a three company front. His engineers used Bangalore torpedoes and satchel charges to neutralize many inland Japanese positions. But the strongpoints along the re-entrant were a deadly and veritable hornet's nest. Light Marine tanks made courageous frontal attacks against the Japanese fortifications. The tanks fired their 37mm guns point-blank at the Japanese fortifications, but were inadequate for the task. One tank was destroyed because of enemy fire, and the other two withdrew. Maj. Hays called for a section of 75mm half-tracks. One half-track was lost instantly, but the others used their more massive guns to considerable advantage.

The left flank and center companies curved around behind the main Japanese strongpoints, cutting the enemy off from the rest of the island. Along the beach, the progress was measured in yards. A small Japanese party tried a sortie from the strong points against the Marine lines. Now the Marines were finally given actual targets in the open—they cut the Japanese down in short order.

Maj. Jones made his final preparations for the assault to the east on Green Beach, with the 1/6 Marines. He had access to several light tanks available from the platoon that came ashore the prior evening. Maj. Jones preferred the medium tanks' effectiveness and borrowed two medium battle-scarred Sherman's from Ryan for the assault. Maj. Jones ordered the tanks to range no further than fifty yards ahead of his lead company. He personally kept in radio contact with the tank commander. Jones assigned a platoon of .30-caliber water-cooled machine guns to each rifle company and attached combat engineers with flamethrowers and demolition squads. Due to the nature of the terrain and the necessity for giving Maj. Hays' battalion a wide berth, Jones constrained his attack to a zone of only one-hundred yards wide. In his words:

This was one of the most unusual tactics I'd ever heard of. As I moved to the east on one side of the airfield, Larry Hays moved to the west of me, exactly opposite.

Maj. Jones' plan was well executed. He had the advantage of a fresh tactical unit in place with integrated supporting arms. The 1/6 Marine landing team made rapid progress along the south coast, killing over two hundred Japanese defenders. American casualties were light at this point, and he reached the thin lines held by the 2/2 and the 1/2 in less than three hours.

Col. Shoup called Maj. Jones to his command post at 1100 to brief him on the afternoon plan of action. Major Jones' XO, Major Francis Beamer, was to take and replace the lead rifle company. Enemy resistance had stiffened, and the company commander had just been shot and killed by a sniper. The oppressive heat was taking its toll on the Marines. While Beamer made superhuman efforts to get more salt tablets and water for his men, several of his troops had fallen out and become victims of heatstroke. First Sergeant Lewis Michelony later wrote:

Tarawa's sands were as white as snow and as hot as red white ashes from a heated furnace.

On Green Beach, only 800 yards behind the 1/6 Marines, the landing team of the 3/6 Marines streamed to shore. While the landing took several hours to execute, it was uncontested. Not until 1100 did Maj. Jones' lead elements link up with the 2nd Marines before the 3/6 were fully established onshore.

The 8th Marines attack order was the same as the previous day: attack Japanese strong points to the east. These obstacles were just as difficult on D+2. Three of the Japanese fortifications were especially formidable:

1. A steel pillbox near the contested pier
2. A large bombproof shelter further inland
3. A coconut log emplacement with multiple machine guns

All three obstacles had been designed by the master engineer, Adm. Saichiro. These strongpoints, mutually supported by fire and observation, had effectively contained the combined Marine forces of the 3/8 and the 2/8 since the assault on D-Day.

Maj. Crowe reorganized his tired forces into another assault.

The former marksmanship instructor got cans of lubricating oil out and made his troops field strip and clean their M1s before the attack. Crowe placed his Battalion XO, Major William Chamberlin, in the center of the three attacking. Chamberlin was a former college economics professor and was no less dynamic than his red mustached commander. Still nursing a painful wound in his shoulder received at D-Day, Chamberlin was a major player in the repetitive assaults against the three Japanese strong points. 1stSgt. Michelony later wrote about Chamberlin:

He was a wild man, a guy anybody would be willing to follow.

Chamberlin took his mortar crew and scored a direct hit on top of the coconut log emplacement at 0930. He penetrated the bunker and detonated the ammunition stocks. It was a stroke of great fortune for the Marines. At the same time, the medium tank *Colorado* penetrated the steel pillbox with its 75mm guns. Now, two of the three emplacements were overrun.

The massive bombproof shelter was still lethal. Flanking attacks were getting shot to pieces before they could gather any momentum. The solution was to get to the top of the sand-covered mound and drop thermite grenades or explosives down the air vents to force the Japanese outside. This formidable task went to Maj. Chamberlin and a squad of combat engineers.

Machine gunners and riflemen opened up a sheet of fire against the strongpoint's firing ports. Chamberlin led a small band and raced across the sands up the steep slope. The Japanese knew they were in mortal danger. Dozens of them poured out of the rear entrance, attacking the Marines on top. A Marine stepped forward and emptied his flamethrower into the onrushing Japanese—then charged them with an M1 carbine. The Marine was shot dead and his body rolled down the slope. But other Marines were inspired to overcome the Japanese counterattack.

The remaining combat engineers rushed to place explosives

against the rear entrances. Hundreds of demoralized Japanese broke out in panic and fled eastward; the Marines shot them to pieces. The tank crew fired one "dream shot" canister round. It killed at least twenty Japanese.

Maj. Chamberlin's bravery resulted in a posthumous Medal of Honor. The third to be awarded to the Marines on Betio. His single-handed sacrifice almost ended the stalemate on Red Beach Three. There's no coincidence that two of these highest awards were received by combat engineers. The bravery and courage under fire represented hundreds of other engineers on only a slightly less spectacular basis. Almost an entire third of the combat engineers who landed in support of the 2/8 ended up as casualties. According to Maj. Chamberlin, his combat engineers used:

Eight cases of TNT, eight cases of gelatin dynamite, and two 54-pound blocks of TNT to destroy Japanese fortifications. The engineers used an entire case of dynamite and both large blocks of TNT to destroy the large bombproof shelter alone.

STRONG RESISTANCE

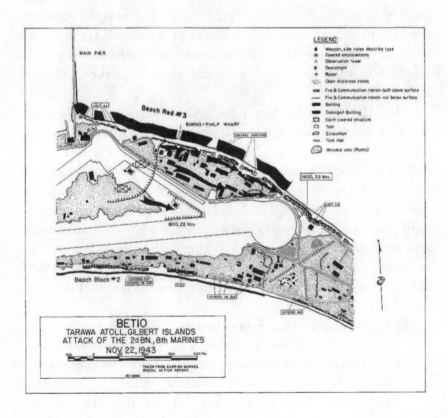

BETIO
TARAWA ATOLL, GILBERT ISLANDS
ATTACK OF THE 2d BN., 8th MARINES
NOV 22, 1943

DURING THE CHAOTIC, murderous fighting in the 8th Marines' zone, Adm. Shibasaki was killed in his blockhouse. The unyielding Japanese commander's failure to provide any backup communications to the above-ground wires, which were destroyed during the preliminary D-Day bombardment, kept him from influencing the battle. The Imperial Japanese archives showed that Shibasaki transmitted one last message to Tokyo early in the morning on D+2:

Our weapons have been destroyed. From now on, everyone is attempting the final charge. May Japan exist for 10,000 years.

Gen. Julian Smith arrived on Green Beach just before noon. Smith conferred with Maj. Ryan and observed the deployment of the 3/6 Marines inland. Gen. Smith realized he was far removed from the main action toward the center of the island. He returned to his landing craft and ordered the coxswain to make for the pier. It was here that the commanding general received his rude welcome to Betio.

Maj. Hays' 1/8 Marines were besieging the Japanese strongpoints at the re-entrant. But the Japanese defenders still had control over the approaches to Red Beaches One and Two. The defenders' well-aimed machine gun fire disabled Smith's boat and killed his coxswain. The other occupants of his group leaped over the gunwale and into the water. Maj. Tompkins, the right man in the right place, waded through Japanese fire for a half-mile to find the general another LVT. This LVT drew fire and wounded the coxswain, further alarming the remaining occupants. Gen. Smith did not reach Col. Edson and Shoup's combined command post until 1400.

In the meantime, Col. Edson had assembled his commanders and issued orders to continue the attack to the east that afternoon. The 1/6 Marines would continue along the narrowing south coast, supported by the howitzers and all available tanks from the 1/10. Col. Hall would lead two battalions of the 8th Marines and continue advancing along the north coast. Air support and naval gunfire would blast the areas for two hours in advance.

Col. Hall spoke up about his exhausted and decimated Marine landing teams. They'd been in direct contact and ashore since D-Day morning. He told Edson the two landing teams had enough strength for only one more assault, and then they must get relieved.

Col. Edson promised to exchange the exhausted 2/8 Marines with the fresh 2/6 Marines on Bairiki at the first opportunity after this assault.

The 1/6 Marines started their attack at 1330. They ran into heavy opposition. They took deadly fire from heavy Japanese weapons mounted in turret type emplacements near the south beach. While this took ninety minutes to overcome, the light tanks were brave but ineffective. It took sustained 75mm fire, from two Sherman medium tanks, to neutralize the Japanese emplacements. Resistance was fierce throughout the zone, and the 1/6 Marines' casualties mounted. They'd taken eight-hundred-yards of enemy territory quickly in the morning, but by the long afternoon had attained half that distance.

The 8th Marines, after having destroyed their three bunker nemesis, made excellent progress at first, but then ran out of steam after they passed the eastern end of the airfield. Col. Shoup was right in his estimation that the Japanese defenders, while leaderless, still had plenty of bullets and fight left.

Maj. Crowe reorganized his leading elements into defensive positions for the night. He placed one company north of the airfield. The end of the airstrip was covered by fire, but unmanned.

On nearby Bairiki Island, the 2/10 Marines fired artillery missions to support Maj. Crowe. Company B of the 2nd Medical Battalion established a field hospital, handling the overflow of casualties. The 2/6 Marines, eager to get into the fight, waited in vain for boats to move them onto Green Beach. Landing craft were mostly unavailable. They were crammed with miscellaneous supplies as the transports and cargo ships continued a general unloading—regardless of the troops' needs ashore.

Navy Seabees on Betio were already repairing the airstrip with bulldozers, under enemy fire. Occasionally, Marines would call in for help from the Seabees to seal up a bothersome bunker. A bulldozer would arrive and do the job nicely.

Shore party Marines and Navy beachmasters on the pier kept the supplies coming in and the wounded going out. Col. Edson requested a working party at 1552 to clear bodies from around the pier that hindered shore party operations.

Later that afternoon the first Jeep got ashore. A wild ride along the pier with every remaining Japanese sniper trying to shoot the driver.

War correspondent Sherrod commented:

If a sign of certain victory was needed, this is it. The jeeps have arrived.

One of Col. Hall's Navajo Indian code-talkers had been mistaken for a Japanese and was shot. This was because of the strain of the prolonged battle. A derelict, blackened LVT drifted onshore filled with dead Marines. At the bottom of the pile was one Marine who was still alive. Still breathing, after two-and-a-half days of an unrelenting hell. He looked up and gasped, "Water. Pour some water on my face, will you?"

Shoup, Edson, and Smith were near exhaustion. While the third day on Betio had been a day of spectacular gains, progress was excruciatingly slow. And the end was not in sight.

Gen. Smith sent this report to Gen. Hermle, who had taken his place on the *Maryland*:

Situation not favorable for rapid cleanup on Betio. Heavy casualties among officers make leadership difficult. Still strong resistance. Many emplacements intact on eastern end of the island. Japanese strong points westward of our front lines within our position have not been reduced. Progress costly and slow. Complete occupation will take at least five days more. Air and naval bombardment a great help but does not take out emplacements.

Gen. Smith took command of operations at 1930. He had seven thousand Marines onshore fighting against one thousand Japanese defenders. Aerial photographs showed many defensive positions were still intact on Betio's eastern tail. Smith believed he would need the entire 6th Marines to complete the job. At 2100 the 6th Marines landed. Smith called a meeting to assign orders for D+3.

The 3/6 Marines would pass through the lines of Maj. Jones' 1/6 Marines to have a fresh Battalion lead the eastward assault. The 2/6 Marines would land on Green Beach and move east to support the 3/6. All available tanks would be assigned to the 3/6. Col. Shoup's 2nd Marines, with the 1/8 still attached, would continue to assault the Japanese re-entrant strongpoints. The remaining 8th Marines would be shuttled to Bairiki. The 4/10 would land its heavy 105mm guns on Green Beach to increase the howitzer battalions' firepower that was already in action.

Imperial Japanese soldiers began vicious counterattacks during the nights of D+2 and D+3. Maj. Jones believed his exposed forces would be the target for any *Banzai* attacks and took his precautions. He gathered his artillery forward observers and naval fire control spotters. Jones arranged for field artillery support starting from seventy-five yards from his front lines to 500 yards out, where naval gunfire would take over. Maj. Jones put Company A to the left of the airstrip and Company B on the right along the south shore; while he worried about the 150-yard gap across the runway to Company C, he realized there was no solution. Jones used a tank to bring up stockpiles of small arms ammunition, grenades, and water to be kept fifty yards behind the lines.

At 1930, the first Japanese counterattack began. Fifty Japanese soldiers snuck past Maj. Jones' outposts through thick vegetation and penetrated the border between the two companies south of the airstrip. Maj. Jones' reserve force was composed of his headquarters' cooks, bakers, and admin people. They contained the penetration and killed many Japanese in the two hours of close-in fighting. Direct and intense fire from the howitzers of the 1/10 and 2/10 stopped the Japanese from reinforcing their penetration. By 2130, the lines were stabilized, and Maj. Jones placed a company one hundred yards to the rear of his lines. All he had left was a composite force of forty Marines.

At 2300, the Japanese attacked Jones' lines again. They made a loud disturbance across from Company A's lines. Clinking canteens against their helmets, taunting Marines and screaming *Banzai*, while a second force attacked Company B in a silent rush. The Marines repelled this attack but used their machine guns, revealing their positions. Maj. Jones requested a full company from the 3/6 to reinforce the 2nd Marines to the rear of the fighting.

The third attack came at 0300. The Japanese moved multiple 7.7mm machine guns into nearby wrecked trucks and opened fire on Marine weapons positions. Maj. Jones called for star shell illumination from the destroyers in the lagoon. A Marine sergeant crawled forward against this oncoming fire to lob grenades into the improvised machine-gun nests. This did the job and silenced the battlefield once again.

Three hundred Japanese launched a frenzied attack at 0400 against the same two Marine companies. The Marines repulsed them with every available weapon. Japanese soldiers were caught in a murderous crossfire from the 10th Marine howitzers. Two destroyers in the lagoon, *Sigsbee* and *Schroeder*, opened up on the Japanese flanks. Waves of screaming attackers took vicious casualties but kept coming. Groups of men locked together in bloodied hand-to-hand combat.

PFC Jack Stambaugh of Company B killed three Japanese soldiers with his bayonet before an officer beheaded him with a samurai sword. Another Marine jumped in and knocked out the Japanese officer with his rifle butt. The acting commander of Company B, First Lieutenant Norman Thomas, reached Major Jones on the field phone and said:

We're killing them as fast as they come at us, but we can't hold out much longer. We need reinforcements.

Maj. Jones replied:

We haven't got them. You've got to hold.

The Marines lost 42 dead and 114 wounded in the wild fighting —but they held. In less than an hour, it was all over. The supporting arms never stopped shooting down the Japanese, either attacking or retreating. Both destroyers emptied their magazines of 5-inch shells. The 1/10 Marines fired over 1,400 rounds that night. As dawn broke, Marines counted over 200 dead Japanese within fifty yards of their lines. An additional 130 bodies laid beyond that range, badly mangled by naval and artillery gunfire. Other bodies laid scattered throughout the Marine lines. Maj. Jones had to blink back his tears of pride and grief as he walked his lines. One of his Marines grabbed his arm and said:

They told us we had to hold, and by God, we did.

COMPLETING THE TASK

JAPANESE COUNTERATTACKS during the nights of November 22 and 23 broke the back of their defense. If they'd remained in their bunkers until the bitter end, the enemy could have taken a higher toll of Marine lives. Rather than facing an inevitable defeat, over 600 Japanese soldiers chose to die by taking an offensive night action.

After the bloody counterattacks during the night, the 2nd Marine Division still had over five more hours of tough fighting on Betio before the island could be conquered. Later in the morning Gen. Smith sent this report to Adm. Hill on the *Maryland*:

Enemy counterattack was defeated decisively. Last night destroyed bulk of hostile resistance. Expect complete annihilation of all enemy on Betio this date. Recommend you and staff come ashore to get information on type of hostile resistance which will be encountered in future operations.

After a preliminary bombardment, the fresh troops of the 3/6 Marines weaved through Maj. Jones' lines and began their attack to the east. The Marine assault tactics were now well refined. The 3/6 Marines made rapid progress, led by tanks and combat engineers with flamethrowers and high explosives. Only one well-armed bunker, along the north shore, provided any substantial opposition.

The 3/6 Marines took advantage of the heavy brush along the south shore and bypassed the obstacle. They left one rifle company to encircle and eventually overrun it. Momentum was with the Marines. The remaining Japanese troops seemed dispirited. By 1300, the 3/6 reached the eastern tip of Betio and inflicted over five hundred Japanese casualties at the loss of only thirty-four Marines.

Lieutenant Colonel MacLeod sent a report that summarized the Japanese defenders' collapse in the eastern zone that followed their counterattacks:

At no time was there any determined defensive. We used flamethrowers and could've used more. Medium tanks were excellent. Light tanks did not fire one shot.

The hardest fighting of the fourth day was on the border of Red Beach One and Two. Col. Shoup directed the combined forces of the 1/8 and 3/2 against the re-entrant strongpoint. The Japanese in these positions were the most disciplined and deadliest on the island. In these bunkers, Japanese anti-boat gunners had thoroughly disrupted over four different battalions' landings and almost killed Gen. Smith the day before. The seaward approaches to the strong-points were littered with bloated bodies and destroyed LVTs.

Maj. Hays finally received his flamethrowers and began the attack with the 1/8 from the east, making steady—painstaking progress. Maj. Schoettel was eager to atone for what may have been perceived as a lackluster performance on D-Day. Schoettel attacked and pressed the assault with troops from the 3/2 from the west and south. Completing the circle, Col. Shoup ordered a platoon of infantry and two 75mm half-tracks out to the reef, keeping the enemy pinned down from the lagoon.

The exhausted Japanese defenders either fought to the end or committed *hara-kiri*. The 1/8 Marines had been attacking this fortified strongpoint ever since the bloodied landing on the morning of D+1. In only forty-eight hours, the 1/8 Marines fired over 55,000 rounds of .30-caliber rifle ammo. The real damage was done by the engineers' special weapons, and by direct fire from the 75mm half-tracks. After the Marines captured the largest concrete pillbox position near the beach, they could approach the remaining bunkers more safely. It was all over by 1300.

When the fighting was still underway, a Navy fighter plane landed on Betio's airstrip and weaved around the Seabee trucks. Marines rushed over to the aircraft to shake the pilot's hand.

At 1245, Adm. Hill and his staff came ashore. The senior naval officers were impressed by the great strength of the Japanese bunker system. They realized the need to reorganize bombardment strategies. Adm. Hill praised the Marines for making such a landing and called Betio a "little Gibraltar."

When Col. Shoup reported to Gen. Smith that the ultimate objectives had been seized, Smith shared the excellent news with Adm. Hill. Between them, they had worked together to achieve this victory. They drafted a message to Adm. Turner and Gen. Holland Smith announcing the end of organized resistance on Betio.

Working parties were organized to identify the dead. Many of the bodies were so severely shattered or burned that it was difficult to distinguish between friend and foe. The stench and decay of death was overwhelming. War correspondent Robert Sherrod wrote:

Betio would be more habitable if the Marines could leave for a few days, and the million buzzards swirling overhead could finish their work.

Chaplains accompanied burial teams equipped with bulldozers. Administrative staff worked diligently to prepare accurate casualty lists. Even more casualties were expected in mop-up operations over the surrounding islands including Apamama, also known as Abemama Atoll. A distressing report was issued that over one-hundred Marines were missing. The changing tides swept many bodies of the assault troops out to sea. One of the first pilots ashore reported seeing dozens of floating corpses miles away over the horizon.

The Japanese defenders were nearly annihilated in the battle. The Marines, supported by carrier aviation, naval gunfire, and Army Air Force units, killed 98% of the 4,836 enemy troops on Betio during the assault. Only seventeen Japanese soldiers were taken prisoner. The only Japanese officer captured in the fighting was Kiyoshi Ota. A thirty-year-old ensign in the *7th Sasebo Special Landing Force*, from Nagasaki. Ensign Ota recounted that the Japanese garrison had expected landings along the southwest sectors instead of the northern beaches. He also believed the reef would have protected the Japanese defenders during the low tide.

Before Gen. Julian Smith announced the Marines' victory at Betio, Gen. Ralph Smith, his Army counterpart, reported: "Makin Taken." In three days of hard fighting over on Butaritari Island, the Army had wiped out the Japanese garrison at the cost of 204 American casualties.

Many exhausted and grimy Marines on Betio had been awake since the night before the landing. Capt. Carl Hoffman later wrote in his memoirs:

There was no way to rest. There was virtually no way to eat. Most of it was close, hand-to-hand fighting, and survival for three and a half days. One of my men mixed me a canteen full of hot water, coffee, chocolate, sugar, he gave it to me and told me he thought I needed something. It was the best meal I'd ever had.

Marines were surrounded by the devastation on Betio after the fighting. Chaplain Willard walked along Red Beach One, now finally clear of enemy pillboxes, and scratched out a note to his wife:

I'm on Tarawa in the midst of the worst destruction I've ever seen. Walking along the shore, I counted seventy-six dead Marines staring up at me, half in and half out of the water. An LVT is jammed against the seawall barricade. Three waterlogged Marines lay dead beneath it. Four others are scattered nearby, and there is one hanging on a 2-foot high strand of barbed wire who doesn't even touch the coral flat at all. What I see in this god-awful place I am certain is one of the greatest works of ruin wrought by any man.

Japanese forces in the Gilbert Islands took a bloody toll from the Marine invasion force. Japanese submarines arrived in the area during D+2. The *I-175* sunk the carrier *Liscome Bay* with a torpedo as the sun rose on November 24 off of Makin. A horrific explosion —the flash was seen at Tarawa, over 90 miles away—the ship sank quickly, taking 644 souls with her to the bottom.

The Marines conducted a flag-raising ceremony later that same morning. There were few surviving palm trees to select as a flagpole.

A field musician played the bugle calls, and Marines all over the island stood and saluted. Each reckoning the cost.

More good news came from the V Amphibious Corps Reconnaissance Company. They had landed on Apamama by rubber rafts from the submarine *Nautilus*. On the night of November 21, while the small Japanese garrison kept the scouts at bay, the *Nautilus* surfaced and fired its deck guns, killing many Japanese defenders—the rest committed *hara-kiri*. After the island was deemed secure, the 3/6 Marines took control of Apamama until other defense forces could arrive.

On November 24, amphibious transports entered the lagoon and loaded Marine combat teams 2 and 8. Many Marines believed going back to a ship, after the carnage of Betio, was like going to heaven. Navy personnel were generous and kind. The Marines were treated to a full-scale turkey dinner served by Navy officers. Many Marines still suffered from post-combat trauma.

The 2nd and 8th Marines were on their way to Hawaii, while the 3/6 Marines were on their way to Apamama. The 2/6 Marines were beginning their long trek through the other islands of the Tarawa atoll. Under Maj. Jones, the 1/6 Marines were the last infantry unit on Betio. Their work was tedious and heartbreaking. They buried the dead, flushed out the last of the diehard snipers, and hosted visiting dignitaries.

Gen. Holland Smith, the V Amphibious Corps commander, flew to Betio on November 24. He spent an emotional afternoon viewing the death and destruction with Gen. Julian Smith. Gen. Holland Smith was shaken by what he'd seen and the Marines' sacrifices on the island. He concluded:

The sight of our dead Marines floating in the waters of the lagoon and lying along the blood-caked beaches is one I will never forget. Over the pitted, blasted island hung a miasma of coral dust and death, nauseating and horrifying.

The generals came upon one site that moved all of them to tears. A dead Marine leaned against a seawall, his arm upright from his body weight. Just beyond his upraised hand on top of the seawall was a blue-and-white flag. A beach marker to direct succeeding waves where to land. Gen. Holland Smith cleared his throat and said, "How can men like that ever be defeated?"

Company D of the 2nd Tank battalion was the designated scout company for Tarawa's 2nd Marine Division. Elements of these scouts had landed on the Buota and Eita Islands while the fighting raged on Betio. The scouts discovered a sizable Japanese force. On November 23, the 3/10 Marines landed on Eita. The battalion's howitzers were initially intended to increase support fire on Betio. When the island finally fell, the artillery turned their guns to support the 2/6 clearing out the rest of the islets in the Tarawa Atoll.

At 0500 on November 24, the 2/6 Marine landing team under Colonel Murray boarded boats from Betio and landed on Buota. Murray moved his Marines at a fierce pace, wading across the sand-spits that joined the succeeding islands. Murray learned from friendly natives that a Japanese infantry force of 175 waited ahead on the larger island of Buariki. The lead elements of the 2/6 caught up with the enemy on November 26. After a sharp fire exchange in thick vegetation, Murray pulled his troops back. He positioned his forces for an all-out assault in the morning.

The November 27, Battle of Buariki was the last engagement in the Gilberts. It was no less deadly than the preceding encounter with the *Special Naval Landing Forces*. Col. Murray assaulted the Japanese defensive positions at dawn. He received supporting fire from Battery G before the lines became too intermingled in the melee.

The fighting was not unlike Guadalcanal: hand-to-hand brawling in the tangled underbrush. The Japanese did not have the elaborate defenses found on Betio. But the Imperial Naval soldiers took advantage of as much cover and concealment as they could. They made every shot count and fought to the death. All 175 of them were killed. Col. Murray's victory came at a high cost. 32 Marines killed and 60 more wounded. The next day, the Marines crossed to the last islet and found no more Japanese defenders. Gen. Julian Smith announced on November 28 that the remaining enemy forces on Tarawa had been wiped out.

Adm. Nimitz had arrived on Betio just before Gen. Julian Smith's announcement. Nimitz noted that the primary Japanese defenses were still intact. He had his staff diagnose the exact construction methods the Japanese used. In less than a month, an identical set of pillboxes and bunkers were built on naval bombardment islands in the Hawaiian island chain.

Adm. Nimitz presented a few of the many to come combat awards to the 2nd Division Marines. The Presidential Unit Citation was awarded to the entire division. Col. Shoup received the Medal of Honor. Maj. Crowe and his XO, Maj. Chamberlin, received the Navy Cross, as well as LtCol. Amey, Maj. Ryan, and Cpl. Spillane-- the LVT crew chief and St. Louis Cardinals prospect, who caught the Japanese hand grenades in midair on D-Day before his luck ran out.

While some senior officers were jealous of Col. Shoup's Medal of Honor, Gen. Julian Smith knew whose strong shoulders carried the critical first thirty-six hours of the assault. Col. Shoup recorded in his combat notebook:

With God and the Navy in support of the 2nd Marine Division, there was never any doubt that we would take Betio. For several hours, however, there was a considerable haggling over the exact price we would pay for it.

SIGNIFICANCE OF TARAWA

THE HIGH COST of the battle for Tarawa was twofold: the Marine casualties in the assault, followed by the nation's despair and shock after hearing the battle reports. At first, the gains seemed small. The "stinking little island" of Betio was eight thousand miles away from Tokyo. But the practical lessons learned in the complexity of amphibious assault outweighed the initial public outrage.

Casualty figures for the 2nd Marine Division and Operation Galvanic were 3,407. There were 1,027 dead Marines and sailors. An additional 88 Marines were missing and presumed dead, and 2,292 Marines and sailors wounded. Guadalcanal's campaign cost a similar number of Marine casualties—but spread over six months.

Tarawa losses happened in 76 hours. The killed to wounded ratio at Tarawa was excessive and reflected the savagery of the fighting. Overall, the casualties among the Marines engaged in the fight was around 19%. A steep but *acceptable* price. Many battalions suffered much higher losses. The 2nd Amphibian Tractor Battalion lost half of their men. This battalion also lost 35 of the 125 LVTs on Betio.

Headlines of "The Bloody Beaches of Tarawa" alarmed the American public. This was partially the Marines' own doing. Many combat correspondents were invited along for Operation Galvanic. They had shared the worst of what Betio had to offer in the first thirty-six hours. They only reported what they had observed. Marine Sgt. James Lucas, whose account of the fighting received front-page coverage in both *The New York Times* and *The Washington Post* on December 4, 1943, read:

Grim Tarawa Defense a Surprise, Eyewitness of Battle Reveals; Marines Went in Chuckling, To Find Swift Death Instead of Easy Conquest.

Remarks made by senior Marines involved in Operation Galvanic to the media did little to help soothe public concerns. Gen. Holland Smith likened the assault on D-Day to Pickett's charge at Gettysburg. Col. Edson said the assault force "paid the stiffest price in human life per square yard" at Tarawa than any other engagement in the Marine Corps' history. War correspondent Robert Sherrod wrote of seeing one-hundred Marines gunned down in the water in five minutes on D+1. It did not help when the Marine Corps headquarters waited an additional ten days after the battle to release the casualty list.

The atmospheres at Pearl Harbor and Washington were tense during this period. General Douglas MacArthur was still bitter that the 2nd Marine Division had been taken from his Southwest Pacific Command. He wrote to the Secretary of War and complained that "these frontal attacks by the Navy, like Tarawa, were unnecessary and a tragic massacre of American lives."

American mothers wrote letters by the hundreds, one accusing Adm. Nimitz of "murdering her son."

Frank Knox, the secretary of the Navy, called a press conference in which he blamed a "sudden shift in the wind" for exposing the reef and preventing reinforcements from landing. Congress began a special investigation. Fortunately, the Marines had General Vandegrift in Washington as the newly appointed 18th Commandant.

Vandegrift, a highly decorated and widely respected veteran of Guadalcanal, reassured Congress and pointed out that "Tarawa was an assault from beginning to end."

The casualty reports were less extraordinary than the American public expected. In an editorial by *The New York Times* on December 27, 1943, the paper complemented the Marines for overcoming Tarawa's sophisticated defenses and zealous garrisons. The editorial warned that any future assaults, in the Marshall Islands, could be even deadlier:

We must steel ourselves now to pay that price.

After the war, the controversy continued when Gen. Holland Smith publicly claimed that Tarawa was a mistake. Adm. Nimitz replied by saying that Tarawa's capture knocked down the front door to the Japanese defenses in the Central Pacific.

Nimitz launched the Marshalls Campaign only ten weeks after the seizure of Tarawa. The photo-reconnaissance and attack aircraft from the captured airfields at Apamama and Betio proved vital.

The battle for Tarawa's capture would become the textbook on amphibious assault to guide and influence all subsequent landings in the Central Pacific. Nimitz believed that the prompt and selfless analysis immediately following Tarawa were of great value. He wrote:

From analytical reports of the commanders and from their critical evaluations of what went wrong, of what needed improvement, and of what techniques and equipment proved out in combat, came a tremendous outpouring of lessons learned.

Many senior officers later agreed that the conversion of the logistical LVTs to assault craft made the difference between victory and defeat on Betio. A further consensus was that the LVT-1s and LVT-2s used in the operation were only marginal against the heavily defensive fire. The LVT-1s (Alligators) needed heavier armament, more powerful engines, auxiliary bilge pumps, self-sealing gas tanks, and wooden plugs the size of 13mm bullets. More importantly, there needed to be more LVTs, at least 300 per division. Col. Shoup wanted to keep the use of LVTs as reef-crossing assault vehicles a secret, but there were too many reporters on the scene.

Naval gunfire got mixed reviews. Marines were enthusiastic about the destroyers' responses in the lagoon but critical about the preliminary bombardment's extent and accuracy—especially when it was ended so prematurely on D-Day. Maj. Ryan later wrote that the significant shortcomings in Operation Galvanic were:

Overestimating the damage that could be inflicted on a heavily defended position by an intense but limited naval bombardment, and by not sending in its assault forces soon enough after the shelling.

Maj. Schoettel later wrote that of the pounding his battalion received from emplacements within the seawall, he'd have recommended a direct fire against the beach by 40mm guns from close-in destroyers. The hasty saturation fires, considered adequate by planners because of strategic surprise, proved virtually useless. Any amphibious assaults against fortified atolls would need sustained, aimed, and deliberate fire.

No one could question the bravery of the aviators who supported the assault on Betio. But many questioned whether they were trained and armed adequately for such a difficult target. The need for closer integration of all supporting arms was clear.

Communications throughout the assault on Betio were terrible. Only the resourcefulness of a few radio operators and the bravery of individual runners kept the assault coherent. The Marines needed waterproof radios. The Navy needed a dedicated amphibious command ship, not on board a major combatant whose massive guns knocked out the radio nets with each salvo. These command ships, the AGC's, would appear later during the Marshalls Campaign.

Other amphibious revisions to the doctrine were immediately enacted. The priority of unloading supplies would become the tactical commander's call onshore, not the amphibious task force commander. Betio showed the critical need for underwater swimmers to stealthily assess and report the surf, beach, and reef conditions to the task force before the landing. This concept was first envisioned by amphibious warfare prophet Major Earl "Pete" Ellis in the 1920s, and quickly came to fruition. Adm. Turner created a fledgling UDT (Underwater Demolition Team) for the Marshall Islands assault.

The Marines also learned that the new medium tanks would become valuable assets with proper combined arms training. Future tank training would now emphasize integrated tank, engineer, infantry, and artillery operations. Tank and infantry communications would need immediate improvement. Most casualties among tank commanders on Betio resulted from individuals needing to dismount their vehicles to speak with the infantry in the open.

Backpack flamethrowers won universal approval from the Marines on Betio. Each commander recommended increases in range, quantity, and mobility for these assault weapons. Suggestions were that larger versions should be mounted on LVTs and tanks, predicting the appearance of "Zippo Tanks" in later Pacific campaigns.

Gen. Julian Smith summed up the lessons he learned at Tarawa with this comment:

We made fewer mistakes than the Japs did.

Military historian Philip A. Crowl wrote in his assessment of the battle for Tarawa:

The capture of Tarawa despite all defects in execution, conclusively demonstrated that the American amphibious doctrine was valid, that even the strongest island fortress could be seized.

Future landings in the Marshall Islands would use this doctrine to achieve objectives against similar targets with fewer casualties and in less time. The benefits of Operation Galvanic quickly outweighed the steep initial costs. In time, Tarawa became a symbol of sacrifice and courage for Marine raiders and Japanese defenders alike.

Ten years after the battle, Gen. Julian Smith saluted the heroism of the Japanese who chose to die almost to the last man. He then turned to his beloved 2nd Marine Division shipmates in Task Force 53 at Betio:

For the officers and men, Marines and sailors, who crossed that reef, either as assault troops, or carrying supplies, or evacuating wounded, I can only say that I shall forever think of them with the feeling of the greatest respect and reverence.

TARAWA TODAY

Decades after World War II, Tarawa remains mostly unchanged. Visiting Betio Island, you can still see wrecked LVTs and American tanks along the beaches as well as ruined Japanese pillboxes and gun emplacements. The imposing concrete bunkers created by Adm. Shibasaki still stand, as impervious to time as they were to the naval guns of Task Force 53. At the turn of the century, island natives found a buried LVT containing skeletons of its Marine crew inside—one Marine still wearing his dog tags.

In 1968, Gen. David Shoup was recalled from retirement to active duty for nine days to dedicate a large monument on Betio. He commemorated the twenty-fifth anniversary of the famous fight and later told *The National Observer*:

My first reaction was that Betio Island had shrunk a great deal. It seems smaller now in peace than in war.

While Shoup toured the ruined fortifications, he recalled the desperate, savage fighting. He pondered why the two nations spent so much for so little. In seventy-six hours of fighting, nearly 6,000 Americans and Japanese died on the tiny island.

In the late 1980s, the American Memorial had fallen into disrepair. It was in danger of being dismantled for a cold storage plant to be used by Japanese fishermen. The 2nd Marine Division Association and Long Beach journalist, Tom Hennessey, began a lengthy campaign to raise enough funds to get a new, more stable monument. They brought a 9-ton block of Georgia granite with the inscription "To our fellow Marines, who gave their all." They dedicated this Memorial on November 20, 1988.

Betio is now part of the Republic of Kiribati. Tourist facilities have been developed to accommodate the large number of veterans who return every year. In author James Ullman's opinion, the small island still resembles what it probably looked like on D-Day almost 78 years ago. Ullman visited Tarawa several years ago and wrote a fitting eulogy:

A familiar irony that old battlefields are often the quietest and gentlest of places. It has been true of Gettysburg, Cannae, Austerlitz, Verdun—and is true of Tarawa.

MAJOR GENERAL JULIAN C. SMITH

THE PINNACLE of Gen. Smith's life and career was the epic battle on Tarawa. At the time of Operation Galvanic, Smith was fifty-eight years old and had been a Marine Corps officer for thirty-four years. He was born in Elkton, Maryland, and was a graduate of the University of Delaware.

He'd served overseas in the expeditionary tours of Nicaragua, Panama, Mexico, Haiti, and Santo Domingo. A Naval War College graduate in 1917, he spent World War I in Quantico, Virginia, with many other frustrated Marine officers.

Smith was a rifle team coach and a distinguished marksman. He had limited experience in the FMF (Fleet Marine Force). He took command of the 5th Marines in 1938 and was ordered to the 2nd Marine Division in May 1943.

Gen. Smith earned the respect of his contemporaries. While modest and humble, he had a fighting heart. Col. Ray Murray described him as a "fine old gentleman of high moral fiber. You'd fight for him."

Smith knew what to anticipate from the neap tides at Betio. In his memoirs, he wrote:

I'm an old railbird shooter up on the marshes of the Chesapeake Bay. You push over the marshes at high tide, and when you have a neap tide, you can't get over the marshes.

Gen. Smith was awarded the Navy Cross for his heroic acts in Nicaragua and the Distinguished Service Medal for his actions on Tarawa. While the balance of his career was unremarkable, he retired in 1946 as a lieutenant general and died at the age of 90 in 1975. He valued his experiences on Tarawa. In one of his last letters, he wrote:

It will always be a source of supreme satisfaction and pride to be able to say I was with the 2nd Marine Division at Tarawa.

COLONEL DAVID M. SHOUP

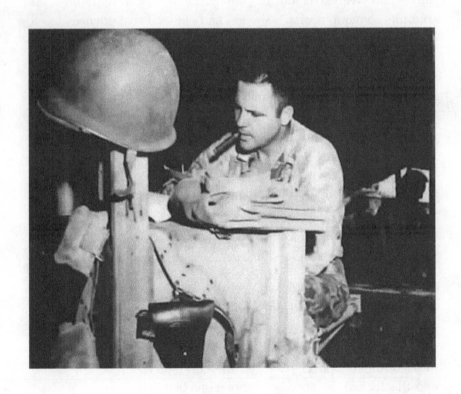

DAVID SHOUP CARRIED a field notebook during the battle of Tarawa. This passage gives us a glimpse into his enigmatic personality:

> *If you are qualified, fate has a way of getting you to the right place at the right time—tho' sometimes it appears to be a long, long wait.*

A farm boy from Battle Ground, Indiana, the combination of time and place benefited Shoup on two momentous occasions: at Tarawa 1943, and as Pres. Eisenhower's selection to make him the 22nd Marine Corps Commandant in 1959.

Col. Shoup had been a Marine officer since 1926 and was thirty-eight years old during the battle of Tarawa. Unlike his colorful contemporaries, Shoup had limited experience as a commander and only the briefest exposure to combat. When Tarawa came, Shoup was a junior colonel in the 2nd Marine Division. He commanded eight battalion landing teams during some of the most savage fighting of World War II.

War correspondent Robert Sherrod later wrote of his impressions of Col. Shoup en route to Betio:

> *This Col. Shoup was an interesting character. A squat, red-faced man with a bull neck. He was a hard-boiled, profane shouter of orders. He carried the biggest burden on Tarawa.*

Shoup was revered by his contemporaries as a "Marine's Marine." Sergeant Edward Doughman served with Shoup in China and on Tarawa. He described him as "the brainiest, nerviest, best soldiering Marine I ever met." Shoup had a reputation for being the most formidable poker player in the entire division because of his eyes that looked like "two burnt holes in a blanket."

Col. Shoup's Medal of Honor citation reflects his strength of character:

Upon arrival at the shore, he assumed command of all landed troops and worked with the rest under constant withering enemy fire. During the next two days, he conducted smashing attacks against incredibly strong and fanatically defended Japanese positions despite heavy casualties and innumerable obstacles.

Shoup was a philosophical man. In his 1943 field notebook, he gave us some of his introspection:

I realize I am but a bit chaff from the threshings of life blown into the pages of history by the unknown winds of chance.

David Shoup lived to the age of 78, dying on January 13, 1983. He was buried at Arlington National Cemetery.

INCIDENT ON D+3

THE LAST DAY of fighting on Betio Island cost 1stSgt. Lewis Michelony his sense of smell. Michelony was a combat veteran of Guadalcanal, a 1/6 Marines member, and a former Atlantic Fleet boxing champion. Later in the Pacific War, he received two Silver Stars for conspicuous bravery. But on D+3, he nearly died.

Michelony was with two other Marines on a routine patrol of the area east of Green Beach. They looked for positions to assign the battalion mortar platoon. Infantry companies had cleared the area the previous morning. Other Marines had passed through the complex of seemingly empty Japanese bunkers without incident. The clearing was littered with Japanese bodies and abandoned enemy equipment. The three Marines threw grenades into the first bunker and encountered no response. All was quiet.

Then—out of nowhere—all hell broke loose. The front bunker opened fire with a machine gun, grenades hailed. In an instant, one Marine died; the second escaped, leaving 1stSgt. Michelony face down in the sand. Michelony dove into the nearest bunker, tumbled through a rear entrance, and landed into what he thought was a pool of water. The dim light of the bunker showed it was a combination of urine, blood, and water. It was a mixture from the dead

Japanese bodies and from some live ones. He spat out the vile liquid in his mouth and realized there were still live Japanese among the dead and decaying. The taste, smell, and fear he experienced inside that bunker nearly overpowered him. In his own words:

Somehow I managed to get out. To this day, I don't know how. I crawled out of that cesspool, dripping wet. The sun-dried my utilities as though they had been heavily starched. But they still stank. For months after, I could still taste, smell, and visualize that scene.

Fifty years later, a retired Sergeant Major Michelony still had no sense of smell.

JAPANESE SPECIAL NAVAL LANDING FORCES

THE FIRST LARGE-SCALE encounter between the US Marines and the Japanese *Special Naval Landing Forces* was at Tarawa. Division staff had warned that the "naval units of this type were more highly trained and had a more remarkable tenacity and fighting spirit than the average Japanese army unit." But even the Marines were surprised at the ferocity of the defenders on Betio.

The Japanese Imperial Marines earned the respect of their US Marine Corps counterparts for their discipline, marksmanship, and proficiency with heavy weapons. The SNLF excelled in small unit leadership, bravery, and a willingness to die to the last man. Maj. Jones, who commanded the 1/6 Marines, had engaged more of the enemy in hand-to-hand combat on Betio than any unit. He later wrote:

These Japs were pretty tough, and they were big, all six feet, the biggest Japs I ever saw. Their equipment was excellent, and there was plenty of surplus found, including large amounts of ammo.

In the early years of the war, the Japanese used their SNLF frequently. In 1941, a force of 5,000 landed on Guam, and another 450 were used to assault Wake Island. A small detachment of 113 were the first Japanese reinforcing unit to land on Guadalcanal, ten days after the American landing.

The *Special Naval Landing Forces* gave a fierce resistance to the 1st Marine Division landings on Tulagi early in the Guadalcanal Campaign. A typical unit comprised of three rifle companies, augmented by antiaircraft and anti-boat guns, coastal defense, field artillery units, and labor troops, and was commanded by a naval captain.

The Japanese defenders on Betio used 7.7mm light machine guns. They integrated these weapons into their fortified defense system of over 500 blockhouses, pillboxes, and other placements. Most Marines faced the Japanese M93 during their landings on the northern coast. It was a 13mm, anti-air, anti-boat heavy machine gun. On many seawall emplacements, these deadly weapons provided flanking fire along the boat obstacles and wire entanglements.

Adm. Shibasaki organized his resistance on Betio for "an overall decisive defense at the beach." His troops fought with great bravery and valor. After seventy-six hours of savage fighting, 4,690 men lay dead. Out of 146 prisoners taken, most were conscripted Korean laborers.

Only seventeen wounded Japanese soldiers surrendered.

THE SINGAPORE GUNS

THE WORLD MEDIA claimed that the four 8-inch naval guns used as coastal defense guns by the Japanese were captured from the British at the fall of Singapore.

British writer William Bartsch visited Tarawa in 1977. Writing in his magazine, *After the Battle*, Bartsch examined each of the four guns and discovered the markings indicating manufacture by Vickers, a British ordnance company. The Vickers company presented Bartsch with records that the four guns were part of a consignment of twelve 8-inch, quick-firing guns, sold in 1905 to the Japanese during their war with Russia.

Further investigation at the Imperial War Museum revealed that no 8-inch guns were captured by the Japanese at Singapore. Tarawa's guns came from an older and far more legitimate transaction with the British.

The 8-inch guns that fired the opening salvo in the Battle of Tarawa were not a factor in the contest. Earlier bombing raids probably damaged their fire control systems. Rapid counter-battery fire from American battleships took out their big guns in short order. Col. Shoup wrote that the 2nd Marine Division was fully aware of 8-inch guns on Betio as early as mid-August 1943.

In contrast, Shoup's division intelligence reports, updated nine days before the landing, discounted any other reports that the guns were 8 inches. They insisted that they were probably no more than 6-inch.

The fact remains that many Marine officers were unpleasantly surprised to experience significant caliber near-misses assaulting the amphibious task force on D-Day.

LVT-2 AMPHIBIAN TRACTORS

THE LVT-2, also known as the Water Buffalo, improved upon the initial amphibious vehicle, the LVT-1, also known as the Alligator. A redesigned suspension system, rubber-tired road wheels, and torsion springs guaranteed a smoother ride and improved stability. The power train was standardized with that of the M3A1 light tank. This gave the Water Buffalo greater power and more reliability than its predecessor. With "W" shape treads, it had better propulsion on land and in the water. Unlike the Alligator, the Water Buffalo was armored, which caused it to weigh significantly more. The Water Buffalo carried 1,400 pounds less cargo than the original LVT-1, but it kept its cargo safe from incoming fire.

In June 1942, the Water Buffalo entered production but did not see combat until Tarawa in November 1943. Marines used a combination of LVT-1s and LVT-2s in the Betio assault. Fifty LVTs used at Tarawa were modified in Samoa just before the battle. They installed 3/8 inch boiler plates around the cab for greater protection against shell fragments and small arms fire. Despite losing thirty vehicles to enemy fire at Tarawa, the improved armor was promising and led to the innovation of further armored LVTs.

The LVT-2(A), Buffalo II, requested by the US Army, was a version that saw limited use with the Marine Corps. The LVT-2(A) had a factory-installed armor plating on the hull and cab to resist heavy enemy machine-gun fire. This LVT version appeared identical to the Water Buffaloes except for the armored drivers' hatches. With armor fortification, the Buffalo IIs could function as assault vehicles in the lead waves of an amphibious landing. When introduced to the Marine operations on New Britain, these armored amphibious vehicles provided an excellent service.

Over 3,000 LVT-2(A)s and LVT-2s were manufactured during World War II. These combat vehicles were valuable assets to the Marine amphibious assault teams throughout the Pacific. They transported thousands of troops and tons of equipment. Still, the LVTs had overall design and operational deficiencies. For example, the vehicles lacked a ramp: all troops and equipment had to be loaded and unloaded over the gunwales. This caused problems in regular use and was hazardous during an enemy opposed landing.

This would be one of the leading factors to further develop amphibian tractors in the LVT family during the war.

SHERMAN MEDIUM TANKS

THE 2ND MARINE Division was assigned one company of M4-A2 Sherman medium tanks for Operation Galvanic. The fourteen tanks were deployed from Noumea in November 1943, onboard the *Ashland*. They joined Task Force 53 en route to the Gilberts. Each of these 34-ton, diesel-powered Sherman tanks were operated by a crew of five. They had a gyro-stabilized 75mm gun and three machine guns. Marines had no opportunity to train or operate with their new offensive assets until the D-Day chaos on Betio.

The medium Sherman tanks joined Wave 5 of the ship-to-shore assault on Betio. The tanks weaved through the gauntlet of Japanese fire without incident. Five were damaged when they plunged into hidden shell craters in the murky water. Onshore, the Marines' lack of operating experience with medium tanks proved costly to the remaining Shermans. Commanders ordered the tanks inland to attack targets of opportunity, unsupported. All but two tanks were quickly knocked out of action. Salvage crews worked non-stop each night, stripping severely damaged tanks to keep the others operational.

The Marines had now learned to use these tanks with an integrated team of covering infantry and engineers. With these new tactics, the Sherman's proved invaluable to Major Ryan's seizure of Green Beach on D+1, attacks on D+2, and the final assault on D+3. Early in the fight, Japanese 75mm anti-tank guns were deadly to the Shermans. But once these enemy weapons were neutralized, the defenders could do little more than shoot out the periscope with sniper fire.

Col. Shoup was disappointed by the squandered deployment and heavy losses of the Shermans on D-Day but was tempered by a subsequent admiration for their tactical role onshore. Shoup also wrote that the "so-called crushing effective medium tanks, as a tactical measure, was negligible in the operation." He believed that no one should place any faith in eliminating fortifications by running them over with a tank.

Marine commanders agreed that the Shermans rendered their light tanks obsolete. Medium tanks were easier to get ashore, and they packed greater armor and firepower. By the war's end, the American ordinance industry had manufactured over 48,000 medium Sherman tanks for use by the Marine Corps and US Army in all combat theaters.

AUTHOR'S NOTE

Building a relationship with my readers is one of the best things about writing.

I occasionally send out emails with details on new releases, special offers, and interesting details I find in my research. If you'd like to be added to my Readers Group, just click here and I'll add you to the list.

Before you go, can I ask you for a quick favor?

Will you leave this book a review?

Reviews are important for authors. They help us sell more books and reach more people. I genuinely appreciate you taking a moment of your time to leave this book an honest review.

Thank you for reading,
Daniel Wrinn

REFERENCES

Information about Operation Galvanic is vast, and the information I gathered for this book came from several sources. The USMC archives maintained by the Washington National Records Group in Suitland, Maryland, were a source of reference information as well as websites, newspaper articles, and even History Channel documentaries.

First-hand accounts, as recorded by the surviving participants, also contributed to my research. I've cited the main reference books used below:

Galvanic: Beyond the Reef—Tarawa and the Gilberts, Nicholas Roland (Naval History and Heritage Command, 2020.)

The Official Chronology of the U.S. Navy in World War II, Robert J. Cressman (Annapolis, MD/Washington, DC: Naval Institute Press/Naval Historical Center, 1999.)

Across the Reef: The Marine Assault of Tarawa, Joseph A. Alexander (Quantico, VA: Marine Corps History Division, 1993.)

History of United States Naval Operations in World War II, Vol. VII—Aleutians, Gilberts and Marshalls, June 1942–April 1944, Samuel Eliot Morison, (Boston, MA: Little, Brown and Company, 1951.)

ALSO BY

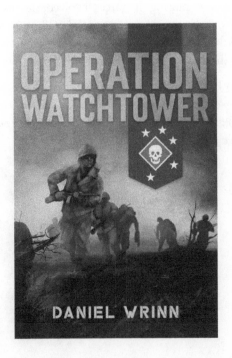

Operation Watchtower

"A terrific read about the pivotal battle on Guadalcanal." – Reviewer

A powerful account of the tide turning WW2 Pacific Theater Campaign.

In the height of the second world war, US forces launched a long and grueling campaign to take the island of Guadalcanal, mounting the first major land attack against Japanese forces. What followed was a 6-month string of devastating battles as these two forces wrestled over this key military position.

In the wake of near-daily aerial attacks and several determined assaults from the Japanese Navy, the Guadalcanal Campaign culminated in a victory for America and marked the first of many offensive attacks aimed at neutralizing the Japanese in the Pacific Theater.

Now, this thrilling book recounts the story of the Guadalcanal Campaign in vivid, gritty detail. Exploring the forces involved, the major battles, and the daily struggle of trying to maintain control of the coveted Henderson Airfield, *Operation Watchtower* examines the pivotal moments which led to the Allies seizing the strategic initiative in a key turning point of the war.

Perfect for fans of WW2 history books covering the Pacific, this brilliant book pays tribute to the brave soldiers on both sides of the conflict, recounting their story for both passionate history fans and anyone searching for an in-depth look at one of the greatest battles of World War II.

9 781393 161240